Hawaiʻi's
PINEAPPLE
CENTURY

Hawai'i's
PINEAPPLE
CENTURY

A History of the Crowned Fruit in the Hawaiian Islands

Jan K. Ten Bruggencate

MUTUAL PUBLISHING

ISBN 1-56647-667-4
Library of Congress Catalog Card Number: 2004104646

Cutout photos on pages i, iii, iv and color insert courtesy of the
DeSoto Brown Collection
Design by Mardee Melton

First Printing, October 2004

Mutual Publishing, LLC
1215 Center Street, Suite 210
Honolulu, Hawai'i 96816
Ph: 808-732-1709
Fax: 808-734-4094
email: mutual@mutualpublishing.com
www.mutualpublishing.com

Printed in Korea

Table of Contents

Foreword

The history of pineapple in Hawai'i parallels the history of the twentieth century in the Islands. Pineapple was one of the two great agricultural industries of the modern era in Hawai'i. It brought employment, altered land use over vast areas, promoted immigration, and created a certain image of the Islands for those abroad. Unlike its older sibling, sugar, which was launched during the early years of the Hawaiian monarchy, pineapple is largely a child of the twentieth century. While settlers from several nations, both European and American, established sugar as a major crop, pineapple was identifiably an American industry. Its development was largely a result of the American influence in the Islands after the 1893 overthrow of the monarchy and Queen Lili'uokalani and the subsequent cession of the new republic to the United States.

The significance of plantations in Hawai'i's development cannot be overstated. Researchers have made much of the modern transformations in the Islands which resulted from the plantation-model—when companies provided for virtually every need of their employees. Plantations supplied housing and medical care, provided retail stores, hired police and meted out justice, maintained the utilities, and offered recreational opportunities. As statehood approached, the strength of the plantations waned under the twin pressures of foreign economic competition and a new domestic political scenario, in which labor interests and the offspring of immigrants gained control of government. Residents now looked to government to provide many of the same kinds of benefits that had been provided by plantations. Hawai'i's state government reflected the top-down management style of plantations, and the state developed one of the most centralized models of state government found in the United States.

In this book, the pineapple industry is chronicled from its earliest days through the modern era. The crop was a fledgling industry with great potential as the century dawned, it survived the Great Depression, thrived in the middle of the century, and then waned as the sun set on the millennium. Only one cannery survived into the twenty-first century, and most of the state's remnant pineapple fields transitioned to fresh fruit production. The colorfully labeled cans of golden fruit could no longer compete with low-cost foreign products.

We have intended, throughout the book, to spell Hawaiian language words and place names with diacritical markings using Pukui and Elbert's *Hawaiian Place Names* as a guide; however, we have chosen to present company names in the way in which the companies themselves spelled them, most often without diacriticals.

The author, a former scientific research director for Libby, McNeill & Libby, arrived at the Libby plantation on the island of Moloka'i in 1956 and remained until Libby closed its Moloka'i operations in 1970. During his career he also worked in pineapple research for U.S. government assistance programs and as an independent consultant in the tropical and subtropical areas of Africa, Asia, and the Americas. He retired while working for Nestlé, growing pineapple in South Florida for the East Coast fresh fruit market. In the preparation of this history, he drew heavily on his personal experience, but also on the input of many people close to the industry.

The archives of the Bishop Museum provided much of the graphic material, and the author thanks the Museum and its collections manager DeSoto Brown. Many photographs and other primary information are from the Libby company files at its Chicago headquarters, which were given to the author when the company closed. The unpublished monograph "By Nature Crowned," by Gus Oehm, which was produced for the Hawai'i Pineapple Research Institute, was also an important research source. Contemporary history of Hawai'i, contained in newspapers like *The Honolulu Advertiser* and the *Honolulu Star-Bulletin*, as well as current periodicals, also aided in the work. The late Pineapple Research Institute plant physiologist and ethnobotanist Beatrice Krauss read and commented on early versions of the book. Any errors or omissions are entirely those of the author and editor.

At Bonita Springs, Florida, and Līhu'e, Hawai'i,
Jan K. Ten Bruggencate, author
Jan W. P. TenBruggencate, editor

Preface

THE MARKETING OF PINEAPPLE
AND OF HAWAI'I

Pineapple has been inextricably linked during much of the twentieth century to the selling of Hawai'i to tourists. Sex has been involved as well, along with surf, and coconuts. There is no end to Hawai'i publicity and advertising photographs of girls in beach or hula attire (or something passing for hula attire), perhaps a palm or two, maybe a sandy shore—and pineapples.

The Islands' larger agricultural industry was sugar, but when it came to marketing the Islands, pineapple held sway over its elder colleague. Sugar, ultimately, was a commodity. Pineapple was something different. It was a fruit with the colors of sunset. It was luscious and juicy. It had that remarkable crown, which led to all kinds of royal metaphors.

Key to pineapple is its inherent opposing yet complimentary characteristics. Its sweetness counters by the tartness of its acids. Its warm color plays against sharp thorns. Other fruits tend to droop down from trees, dangling precipitously, helpless in the grip of gravity—but the pineapple rises up from a sheaf of swordlike leaves growing low to the ground, defying gravity until fully ripe and so heavy that it leans for support on the stiff blades of its foliage.

By the standard of most North American fruits, the pineapple was huge. In a world familiar with apples and oranges, blueberries and grapes, there must have been a sense of intrigue about a fruit the size of a human head, whose stalk was at one end and which had greenery at the other.

Pineapple can label.

Pineapple, in a word, was exotic. And that was just the characteristic that the visitor industry wanted to convey about the Islands.

Pineapple captured the imagination of a nation, of a world, and helped create one image of the Hawaiian Islands.

Jamaica had rum.

Tahiti had Paul Gaugin.

Hawai'i had pineapple.

And, of course, pretty girls, pristine beaches, and coconut palms.

It is not entirely clear whether pineapple was more important to the selling of Hawai'i for tourism, or whether Hawai'i was the feature that sold the pineapple. But the pineapple industry wasted no time in linking its products to the Islands.

The establishment in 1908 of the Association of Hawaiian Pineapple Growers launched the first industry-wide marketing program for the fruit. Hawaiian pineapple began gracing the pages of Mainland U.S. magazines.

In the first decade or so, the growers sold quality. Advertisements extolled the superior features of Hawaiian fruits—as opposed to those grown elsewhere. "It emphasized that Hawaiian pineapple was superior and others inferior," said DeSoto Brown, collections manager with the Bishop Museum archives. "Initially, they don't emphasize exotic scenes with a lot of Island imagery." But by the end of the first third of the century, that was changing.

"Gradually, they started to shift," Brown said, "from text products and stark images of pineapple plants and cans to scenes that integrated pineapple into scenarios depicting the Hawaiian environment—however stylized and historically flawed that environment was." During the 1930s, the hula girls, surfers, and Hawaiian royal court scenes graced much of pineapple's advertising. Never mind that Hawai'i's monarchy had been overthrown, or that the artists' renderings often showed Hawaiians with brown skin but distinctly European features. The Islands and pineapple, after all, were to be seen as exotic, but not too exotic.

In the 1930s and again in 1951, Dole offered stylized maps of the Islands, which were mailed to customers who requested them. The maps familiarized Mainlanders with the configuration of the state, the fact that there were numerous Islands—not just Honolulu-Waikīkī—and that the place had a level of complexity. Besides the beaches, there were mountains, there was agriculture, there was culture, even fishing. And—more importantly—planes and boats went there.

The product was marketed through the major producers—Dole, Libby's, Del Monte, and the rest—but a key feature of pineapple distribution was the private label. Literally dozens—perhaps hundreds—of different labels were used. And   as varied as their names were the images they carried—beaches, hula girls, red anthurium leaves, royalty, flowers. Some brands were named after the stores or the chains of stores where they were sold. Many had English names, but a remarkable number used Hawaiian words, like Hala Brand, which uses a part of the Hawaiian name for pineapple, *hala kahiki*. The key feature in most of these labels was the reference to Hawai'i. The Islands had carefully nurtured the cachet.

Even after most of the pineapple fields closed, and only one firm, Maui Land and Pine, was still selling canned Hawaiian fruit, the connection to the Islands was still important. Each can is labeled "100% Hawaiian U.S.A." On its Web site, Maui Land and Pine includes a logo with the words: "100% Hawaiian Pineapple Rules"—and informs readers that Dole and Del Monte canned products come from the Philippines and Thailand.

After all, there is Hawaiian pineapple first, and then there is everything else.

Field worker in the 1920s marks the locations of pineapple beds in preparation for planting.

The Early Years

Pineapple is a fruit of the New World. It takes its scientific name, *Ananas*, from the language of the Guarani Indians of Paraguay. Their word *anana* means "excellent fruit." Columbus discovered pineapple during his second voyage to the Americas in 1493 when he anchored off Guadeloupe in the West Indies. Later, the Spanish reported finding pineapple in the Philippines, but it is thought that Magellan may have introduced the fruit there on his arrival in 1521. Western ships also reported finding pineapple in the Marquesas, the island chain that is now the northernmost part of French Polynesia. These fruits may be the result of early European contact as well, or could, like the sweet potato, have been the result of contact between Polynesians and the American natives before European presence in this part of the Pacific.

Many botanists believe the pineapple was brought to Hawai'i by a European ship after the arrival of Capt. James Cook, but there is no known record of that first plant appearing on Hawaiian shores. Europe was already familiar with the fruit by the time of first contact in Hawai'i. However, the crop was established in Hawai'i so early that it remains possible it preceded Cook to the Islands. Polynesian settlers from the

Marquesas Islands, or perhaps Spanish contact before the arrival of Cook in 1778, may have brought plants to Hawai'i, which would account for the Wild Black Spanish and the Wild Kailua varieties that were noted growing mainly on Hawai'i's Kona Coast shortly after Cook's arrival.

Pineapple was being moved aggressively around the globe in the 1700s and 1800s. From the end of the 16th century, pineapple could be found growing in India, Java, and in hothouses in Europe, where the Queen variety was the most favored. The crop was raised commercially for sale as fresh fruit in Azores hothouses in 1863, the first plants having been brought there from a hothouse in France.

That same year, pineapples were introduced to the Florida Keys. Growers imported soil, since the crop did not grow well on the sandy coral ground of the islands. The crop was moved to the Florida mainland, and a fresh market industry flourished there from 1890 to 1910. A 1917 freeze killed much of the crop, and by 1936, commercial pineapple had disappeared from Florida.

Whether Hawai'i's first pineapple arrived with Polynesian settlers, from the Spanish (there are records of Spanish shipwrecks during the two centuries before Cook), or whether it arrived shortly after Cook, it quickly became a prized commodity. It was grown largely in small domestic patches at first, and the missionaries who arrived in 1820 made references to the fruit. The first written record is the diary of Francisco de Paula Marin, the Spaniard who introduced many plants to Hawai'i.

Marin, called Manning by sailors and Manini by Hawaiians, was born in Jerez, Spain, in 1774. How and when Marin arrived in Hawai'i is a little unclear. He worked for the Spanish in the Americas, but deserted and arrived in Hawai'i

FRANCISCO DE PAULA MARIN

The only available likeness of Marin appeared as an isolated figure in an engraving depicting the tripartite conference that brought together the Hawaiian chiefs, Captain Abel du Petit-Thouars of the French navy's ship La Vénus, *and Captain Edward Belcher of the British warship* Sulphur *on July 21, 1837. An enlargement of a portion of this engraving is shown to the left. The original appeared in Abel du Petit-Thouar's* Voyage Autour du Monde Sur la Frégate La Vénus, Pendant les Années 1836–1839, Paris, 1841.

either in 1793 or 1794 aboard the English ship *Jackall* or the American ship *Lady Washington.* He served Kamehameha and sometime before 1807 settled on Oʻahu, where he began an active agricultural life.

His property covered the block between present-day River Street, Kukui Street, and Maunakea Street. Marin's journal for January 21, 1813, says, "This day I planted pineapples and an orange tree." On June 19, 1819, he wrote, "Today BOQ [Boke, the governor of Oʻahu under Kamehameha II and Kamehameha III] was very sick. I sent to the minister a barrel of taro, six bottles of lemon-juice, five gallons of vinegar, seven pineapples and a barrel of Poe [poi]." Mid-June is the start of the natural ripening period for pineapple, and would be a time when he had the fruits available. When a Mr. C. S. Stewart visited Marin's Honolulu vineyard in about 1829, he reported that it was skirted with pineapples in different stages of maturity. Marin died in 1837 at age sixty-four, after forty-three years in Hawai'i.

Pineapple continued to appear in documents about Hawai'i in the years leading up to 1882. U.S. Navyman Charles Wilkes wrote in 1840, "Pineapples being planted among the lava rocks" on the island of Hawai'i and "the whole settlement (Hilo) forms a pretty cluster; the path and roadsides are planted with pineapples."

In the middle of the century, there was active shipment of the fruit between the Islands and California. Twelve thousand pineapples were shipped between August 28, 1849 and August 10, 1850 from Lahaina, Maui, to California. The next year the number jumped to 21,310 fruits shipped from several islands: 14,310 from Lahaina, 2,000 from Waimea on Kaua'i and Ni'ihau, and 5,000 from Hilo.

Other references indicate the popularity of pineapple in the islands. An 1856 reference says that the tedious ocean crossing from Ni'ihau to O'ahu prevented Ni'ihau's pineapple crop from supplementing apparent shortages of the fruit on O'ahu, which is not believed to have been a major growing center in these years. And, whaling ships in Hilo in 1854 were paying 28 cents a piece for pineapples, and bought 1,380 of them.

The French ship, *Lion*, arrived from Tahiti in 1857, and dumped a load of spoiled pineapples in a weed patch on Hawai'i. Someone reportedly salvaged crowns from some of the rotted fruits and managed to get them growing. That same year, three hundred plants were imported from the Marquesas and planted on east Maui.

In 1882, the industry began seriously heating up with the advent of the canning of pineapple.

The first to venture into commercially canning the fruit were two entrepreneurs named Ackerman and Muller in North Kona, Hawai'i. They used the local small fruit known as Wild Kailua. They peeled the fruit by hand, sliced and sugared it, and cooked it on a kitchen stove. The men formed the cans by hand, soldering the sides and lids, then affixed labels and packaged the cans in crates.

The men shipped samples of sliced, canned pineapple to the Honolulu newspaper, the *Advertiser*, which reviewed it favorably: "The fruit thus prepared we found of excellent flavor and would take first place in any market. Everyone wishes success to Messrs. Akerman [sic] and Muller in this endeavor to turn to account one of the neglected resources of the country." They shipped the cases of pineapple to agents Theo H. Davies & Company, but the firm was unable to find a buyer. They were a little early. Several years later, Ackerman and Muller were asked to provide 1,000 cases, but by that time they had given up the venture.

Capt. John Kidwell, a horticulturist, arrived in Hawai'i in 1882 at the age of thirty-three. He was urged to enter the pineapple business by Charles Hansen, a banana shipper with markets in California. Hansen said he wanted to add pineapple to his fruit shipments. Kidwell acquired pineapple slips in Kona, Hawai'i, and planted them in a farm plot in Mānoa Valley, O'ahu—on the site now occupied by the University of Hawai'i Mānoa Campus. His was a better, bigger variety, and Kidwell is believed to have imported some. By 1885, Kidwell probably was growing the Smooth Cayenne variety, the same variety grown today.

There are conflicting stories about how the Smooth Cayenne variety first found its way to Hawai'i. W. E. Purvis, another grower, apparently independently imported Smooth Cayenne pineapples about the same time as Kidwell and harvested his first crop in 1887. His plants are believed to have come from the Kew Gardens in England. Smooth Cayenne had been mentioned in English publications as early as 1842. Purvis, who lived at Kukuihaele on Hawai'i, and farmed on the Hāmākua Coast, brought in three varieties from Kew: twelve Sugar Loaf, twelve Ripley Queen and twelve Smooth Cayenne. In his tests, the Smooth Cayenne turned out best. To add to the controversy, Thrum's *Hawaiian Almanac and Annual* of 1909 credited Edward Lycan of Madeira with bringing in the first Smooth Cayenne on the ship *City of Paris* in 1884. While Purvis and Lycan may also have brought fruit into the Hawaiian Islands about the same time, Kidwell is generally credited with bringing in the first samples of the Smooth Cayenne variety.

Ten years after his arrival in the islands, Kidwell's plantation had 50,000 pineapple plants. It was 1892, the year pineapple canning began in earnest in Hawai'i. The canning expert was John Emmeluth, who had arrived in Honolulu from Cincinnati in 1879. Emmeluth had gotten into the sheet metal business with the purchase of a store in 1881, where he initially "employed a staff of competent men in sanitary plumbing, of which they made a specialty." The next year, he and Kidwell were discussing building a factory where fruit would be both canned and preserved in glass containers.

Emmeluth had been experimenting with the canning of pineapple since 1889, both in Kona and in Honolulu. He had done some shipping, but wasn't making money. He shipped several lots of between six dozen and two hundred fifty dozen three-pound cans to San Francisco, New York, Boston, and Victoria, British Columbia. Some of the fruit was sliced and some whole, but the market seemed to prefer whole fruit. The pineapple sold for $2.15 to $2.35 per dozen cans, and Emmeluth got a net return of 96 cents to $1.15 on a dozen cans.

He ended up losing $400 of a $2,000 investment in the business. Then he went into partnership with Kidwell.

The men started a plantation at 'Ewa, O'ahu, in 1892. It was called Hawaiian Fruit and Packing Company, and was capitalized with $40,000. The company drilled an artesian well, installed a pump, and built a cannery at Apokaa, near Waipahu. Their goal was to can ten thousand fruits in 1893, but they weren't ready in time. Kidwell cut back his exports from the Mānoa plantation to more quickly develop the 'Ewa fields. In 1893, the men planned to plant one hundred thousand plants, using both the Queen and Smooth Cayenne varieties. In 1894, they planned to plant two hundred thousand plants. The company grew quickly. The first "pack" came out of the factory in 1895. Hawaiian Fruit and Packing shipped 486 cases of two dozen jars on November 13 of that year aboard the *S.G. Wilder*. The total output for the year was five thousand cases, half of it sliced pineapple and half grated. By the time Hawaiian Fruit and Packing was sold in 1898, it had shipped fourteen thousand cases of pineapple and had sold four hundred thousand fresh fruits.

Others were getting into the business during these years. *The Pacific Commercial Advertiser* in 1906 reported that a Canadian farmer had arrived in Hawai'i in 1891 looking for business. He was urged to try pineapple and to grow it on land available from the O'ahu Railway. He created a stock company, the first Pearl City Fruit Company (PCFC), whose partners included Charles T. Wilder, W. C. Weedon, James Lyle, D. McLean, and others. O'ahu Railway gave them liberal terms on land and freight. The farmer imported planting material and his first field contained twenty-five thousand plants. The company started as a fruit producer, but later bought Kidwell's canning plant and remained in business for twenty-eight years.

Chapter One

California fruit grower Byron O. Clark showed up in Hawai'i in September 1897. He was forty-two and had become interested in Hawai'i after reading an 1893 bulletin written by commissioner of agriculture Joseph Marsden. Marsden lauded Hawai'i's potential as a place to conduct agriculture. He spoke particularly of agricultural land that was available at low cost for homesteading.

James D. Dole, one of the towering figures in Hawaiian pineapple, had also read the promotional material. He arrived in November 1899. Dole said:

> From reading the stuff you got the notion that life in Hawai'i on a coffee plantation was just one long, sweet song. I had an idea that after two or three years of reasonable effort, expended on cheap government land, I would be able to spend the rest of my life in a hammock, smoking cigars rolled from tobacco grown on my own place, and generally enjoying a languorous life of ease and plenty.

The government did make land available. The land act of 1895 included a stipulation that a piece of land near Wahiawā on O'ahu would be sold once its lease ran out. Land in Hawai'i was largely held by a few and was already expensive. This parcel of government land would be sold to an association of settlers if they agreed to live on the land and cultivate it for at least three years. The Hawaiian monarchy had been overthrown two years earlier, and there was anticipation that the United States of America might annex Hawai'i and negate the legislation. Byron Clark, though a newcomer, had been appointed secretary and commissioner of agriculture of the Hawaiian Republic. He decided to act before annexation occurred. He got in touch with several acquaintances from California and organized a group to homestead the Wahiawā property. They called themselves the Wahiawā Colony Tract. Clark signed an agreement with the government, which declared the plateau between the Wai'anae Mountains and the Ko'olau Mountains, the two chains that form the island of O'ahu, agricultural land suitable for homesteading. The land was divided into parcels. The first group of settlers left California in August 1898, bringing with them household goods, horses, livestock, chickens, and even some citrus trees. They moved directly to Wahiawā on their arrival in Honolulu, and appeared pleased with what they found. Thirteen families comprising eighty people formed the initial group of settlers. They took up residence on sixteen farms that ranged from 50 to 250 acres. Clark did not want to appear to be taking advantage of his position, so he had fourth choice of property. The first three would all later play important roles in the development

THE WAHIAWĀ COLONY TRACT
From Public Land Map #25 (1899).

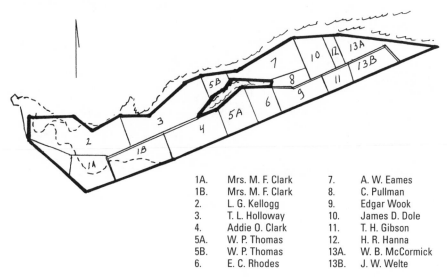

1A.	Mrs. M. F. Clark	7.	A. W. Eames
1B.	Mrs. M. F. Clark	8.	C. Pullman
2.	L. G. Kellogg	9.	Edgar Wook
3.	T. L. Holloway	10.	James D. Dole
4.	Addie O. Clark	11.	T. H. Gibson
5A.	W. P. Thomas	12.	H. R. Hanna
5B.	W. P. Thomas	13A.	W. B. McCormick
6.	E. C. Rhodes	13B.	J. W. Welte

Workers use planting material already laid out on beds as they
build double rows of pineapples on a new field.

of the Hawaiian pineapple industry. They were A. W. Eames, W. B. Thomas, and Leonard C. Kellogg. The land cost was based on the distance from town. Eames got 100 acres a mile east of Wahiawā for $4 an acre. Land nearer the town went for $5 an acre, and land beyond Eames was sold at $3 an acre. James Dole arrived after the first group. He bought 61 acres near Eames and paid $4,000 in 1900.

The Wahiawā land was covered with wild grass and guava, but no large trees. Tilling the soil for the first time and building a home on the site was demanding work. Having it cleared cost more than the settlers paid to buy the land—clearing and ploughing cost $15 to $25 an acre. The farmers knew nothing about growing crops in Hawai'i, and they got no help from veterans like the Chinese vegetable farmers near Honolulu. Because of their lack of knowledge, and their trial and error learning experience, they were called the "Children of the Dark."

By 1900, 400 acres were ploughed and planted with bananas, citrus, pineapple, and other crops. The farmers had fifteen hundred orange trees in the ground and ten thousand in the nursery, forty thousand pineapple plants, three thousand banana plants, and several thousand miscellaneous fruit trees.

The settlers were isolated, 25 miles from Honolulu. They desperately needed a road and a good bridge over the gulch. They had 300 acres at the present site of Wahiawā town designated for settler homes, and, slowly, their community built itself. By 1901 a road had been built from Wahiawā through the farm lots to the foot of the Ko'olau Mountains. It was called California Avenue. There was a school, Sunday school, a post office, store, and social and book clubs. Sometime after 1906, a hotel was built in Wahiawā and operated for several years.

In 1906, the homesteaders were carting their produce 7 miles to the Waialua railroad station, or 10 miles to the railway station in Pearl City. They were required to guarantee the railway company that they would ship at least 20,000 tons of goods annually by 1909 in order to get a branch line built to Wahiawā.

Leonard Kellogg led the effort to bring water to the fields. The group organized a water company, and in 1902, a ditch from Kaukonahua Stream in the Koʻolaus was completed at a cost of $80,000. A third of the water was for the homesteaders and two-thirds was assigned to the Wahiawā Agricultural Company. The ditch had 1,500 feet of open waterway in a total length of 3 ¾ miles. The waterway had thirty-seven tunnels, the longest 1,858 feet long, and five others of more than 1,000 feet.

By the end of 1906, the Wahiawā growers had 5.5 million pineapple plants on 1,100 acres. Fresh pineapple was shipped all over the United States. The San Francisco price was 4 to 5 cents a pound.

The first major cannery was Kidwell and Emmeluth's 1895 Apokaʻa plant, west of Waipahu. Byron Clark started canning in his kitchen and the operation took over his whole house. But James Dole built the second commercial cannery in Hawaiʻi in 1902. Clark followed with a cannery built in Wahiawā in 1905, and Eames built one in Wahiawā in 1906. W. B. Thomas built the sixth plant the same year.

Thomas wrote an article in the *Paradise of the Pacific* about the situation:

> Between Pearl City and Waialua, with the Koʻolau mountains on the east and the Waianae mountains on the west, lies a valley, almost twenty miles long and from eight to ten miles wide. Almost midway

and at the highest point in the valley, between the two towns named, is Wahiawā, where is located the Wahiawā Colony or what is often called the California Colony. The settlement is on a tract of land containing about 1,500 acres, three and a half mile long and from one-half to one mile wide extending from the government road on the west to the Koʻolau mountains on the east, between the north and south branches of the Kaukonahua river. Considerable interest attaches to this colony, as it represents the first systematic effort ever made on the island of Oʻahu by a party of people in one community to demonstrate what can be done in the way of growing miscellaneous farm crops and fruits. As its name implies, the colony is largely composed of residents of California, who have had years of practical experience in fruit growing in the state.

He went on to complain that "King Sugar" had taken up most of the agricultural land, and that the Wahiawā land was all that had been available. But Wahiawā, Thomas wrote, was a paradise:

As a suitable place of residence no more charming spot could be found the world over than Wahiawā. The climate the year round is simply perfect. Its elevation is from 800 to 1,200 feet and this removes it from the extremes of heat felt at lower levels during the summer, and the morning and evenings in the winter are just cool enough to exhilarate. As for scenery, it would be hard to imagine a lovelier vista. In the rivers that border the settlement are numerous fine fishing pools, most phlegmatic to a plunge. A splendid trail has been cut into the hitherto inaccessible forests of the Koʻolau mountains, and as it winds in and out, scenes are unfolded in rapid succession that are almost dazzling in grandeur.

Diorama of a Hawaiian pineapple plantation, with bananas in the foreground, prepared by Libby for the 1933 World's Fair.

The Pioneers

Hawai'i's pineapple industry would not have taken root and flourished without the efforts of pioneers who contributed efficient and cost effective ways to grow, harvest, preserve, ship and market the exotic fruit. This chapter outlines in reference form significant figures in the establishment of pineapple as an economically viable industry in Hawai'i. The pioneers are presented in the general chronological order in which they got involved in pineapple production.

Ackerman and Muller were the first known canners of pineapple in Hawai'i. Their venture, mentioned earlier, was reported in the *Advertiser* in 1882 and repeated in the August 22, 1932 publication, *History from the Advertiser Files*.

Charles Wilcox began to grow pineapples on Maui in 1888, according to an article written by John Emmeluth. Wilcox was a major shipper of fresh pineapple to California by the year 1892. He grew twenty-thousand Wild Kailua pineapples at Mākena on the island's south coast. In 1892, he added fifteen thousand plants, of which ten-thousand were native and five thousand of a variety imported from Mexico. He planned another sixty thousand plantings during the subsequent two years. Wilcox shipped eight thousand fruit in 1891 and twenty-three thusand in 1892, all during the crop's natural fruiting period of June to early September. His average return was 8 cents a fruit, after various charges were subtracted. The price was highest at the start and end of the season. Mid-season fruits were sold at a loss.

Dwight David Baldwin, the son of missionary Dwight Baldwin, was born in 1831, the year his parents arrived in Hawai'i. He and his brother Henry grew sugar cane in Lahaina after 1863. He became manager of the Kohala Sugar Company and held the post for seven years. In 1873, at age 42, Baldwin moved to New England and became librarian at the College of New Haven in Connecticut (now Yale University). He was back in Hawai'i the next year, when King Kalākaua named him inspector general of public schools. In 1890, Baldwin, fifty-nine, was back on Maui and seriously experimenting with commercial pineapple production. He grew the Wild Kailua variety, buying his planting material from O'ahu growers Kidwell, Camarinos, and the Jordan brothers. Baldwin sold his fruit on the local market at first, then began exporting to California. He continued growing pineapple through 1900, when he was sixty-nine.

Captain John Kidwell was born in Devonshire, England, in 1849. He learned agriculture at a nursery near London, where he had been apprenticed at age fifteen to a distant Scottish relative. He was a hard worker and shortly was earning a man's wages. He moved to San Francisco in 1872 and started a nursery. Because of the year of his birth, he jokingly called himself a forty-niner—but he was far too young to have participated in the gold rush whose prospectors took that nickname. It was never clear where he got the title "captain." It's possible he went to sea during his ten years in California, or he could have been a member of some volunteer force in the city. In any case, he met the wife of J. Mott-Smith, the Hawaiian Kingdom's minister in Washington, and she urged him to move to Honolulu and start a nursery. He obtained letters of introduction to several important people in Hawai'i, and sailed for the Islands in 1882. With Charles Hansen marketing his fruit, Kidwell started with Wild Kailua plants obtained from Kona, Hawai'i. His Mānoa plantation was the first serious commercial pineapple farm. Hansen died shortly after their arrangement got started, and Kidwell took to selling the fruit in Hawai'i and later established an export market to California.

Kidwell recognized the problem of the small fruit size of the Wild Kailua and reported that he was soon "skirmishing for plants and slips." After searching nurserymen's periodicals and other publications, he finally learned of a Florida variety new to him called Smooth Cayenne. He wrote for a dozen plants at first, and in 1886, ordered one thousand more from Jamaica, of which six hundred grew. Still experimenting, he ordered thirty-one different varieties from various sources. Smooth Cayenne was again among them, and he found it to be the outstanding variety of the group.

Kidwell put his nursery background to use and developed a propagation facility in an old house on Beretania Street in Honolulu. He installed chimney pipes in the soil to provide bottom heat and in the warmed soil placed old pineapple stumps, which he laid on their sides and turned from time to time to get them to produce more slips. He was able to obtain fifteen to twenty usable slips—the miniature plants that form as side shoots on a mature plant—from each stump.

California, the main market for exported Hawaiian fresh pineapple, was many days and sometimes weeks away by ship, and buyers complained that the pineapple often arrived in poor condition. Growers were looking for a way to preserve their crops so shipping delays would not affect them so badly. Kidwell teamed up with canning pioneer Emmeluth, and the two of them got Lorrin A. Thurston involved. The Hawaiian Fruit and Packing Company was established in

1892, with Kidwell as president and Emmeluth as treasurer. They started with 145 acres and one hundred thousand plants from Kidwell's Mānoa property. The William Dimond Company sold the first pack from the new Apoka'a cannery to San Francisco in 1895. But profit was a problem, largely because of a 35 percent duty on preserved goods entering the United States. In 1898, Kidwell decided to take a shot at the other major agricultural crop in Hawai'i, sugar, which he anticipated would be more profitable. He sublet his pineapple fields to the 'Ewa Sugar Company and opened the Apokaa Sugar Company. The pineapple cannery was sold in 1899 to the Pearl City Fruit Company, which since 1890 had been growing pineapple for the fresh fruit market. The 35 percent tariff was dropped the same year Kidwell sold the cannery.

Kidwell retired before spending much time in his new agricultural venture. He had been working since age fifteen and decided to have some fun. "I started early and I quit early," he said. He traveled the world, never married, and kept his Honolulu home surrounded by flowers. But he still did some unpaid consulting. Years afterward, W. A. Baldwin told a Hawaiian Pineapple Packers Association conference that Kidwell had visited the Baldwin factory and taste-tested some canned pineapple. "Baldwin, you are packing sawdust and water. . . . If you want to pack some good stuff, you pack it in pineapple juice," Kidwell told him. It took four years before Baldwin took the advice, and it made all the difference, he said.

John Emmeluth had arrived in Hawai'i in 1879, three years before Kidwell. He started as manager of a sheet metal company and eventually bought the business, which had offices at Nu'uanu and Merchant Streets. He later moved to 227-229 King Street, where he had a three-story building. Emmeluth canned and shipped some pineapple, but lost money. However, there was a market. Agents in the United States on both coasts told him that if costs were kept down, there could be an unlimited demand for pineapple. "C. Brewer and Company advised him that they could place a shipload every three months in Boston alone, provided a good article is furnished," reported Lorrin Thurston in *Planter's Monthly*. Based on the prices quoted by the Mainland buyers, Emmeluth figured that even after paying the high U.S. duty, he could make a little money. But if the duty were removed, pineapple could produce a substantial profit.

While Emmeluth was involved in the establishment of the first Hawaiian commercial pineapple cannery, with Kidwell and silent partner Thurston, it is not clear how long he remained associated with the Apoka'a factory and Hawaiian Fruit and Packing Company. By 1898, Emmeluth referred to the firm without mentioning his own involvement, but he remained in close touch with the industry. In an 1897 publication, he listed data on the export of fresh pineapple from Hawai'i: 1891, 5,368 fruit at $2,360; 1892, 40,170 at $10,139; 1893, 19,042 at $10,365; 1894, 44,903 at $9,889; 1895, 65,213 at $8,783; 1896, 147,451 at $15,350; 1897, 116,715 at $14,423.

Emmeluth's writings also cast doubt on the common belief that Kidwell brought in the first Smooth Cayenne plants. He says Kidwell got his first plants of this variety from ones that had been brought in and abandoned by Lycan. In 1898 Emmeluth wrote: "Mr. Lycan imported several hundred smooth leaf Cayenne plants which he planted at Kalihi, on this island. On his removal to the States, the plants were disposed of to different parties and became the nucleus of some of the more pretentious pineapple ranches of today." In addition, T. G. Thrum's *Hawaiian Almanac and Annual* of 1909 reports: "Smooth Cayenne pineapples were introduced by Edward Lycan from Madeira per 'City of Paris' on June 13, 1884. From this has grown the pineapple industry of the present proportion in these islands." The 1884 ship also carried immigrants to Hawai'i from the Azores.

Whether Kidwell or Lycan brought the variety in first, it was clear that Kidwell did the most with it. Emmeluth, in an 1897 reference, wrote, "The first person to make the cultivation of pineapple a specialty, and for that reason a success, is John Kidwell, who has a ten-acre patch at Manoa, near Honolulu, and is interested in the ranch at Apoka'a."

Emmeluth, in 1905, recognizing the danger to the pineapple industry's future because of its fragmentation, suggested in a letter to the *Hawaiian Forester and Agriculturist* that the growers form an organization, "in the hope that it may assist in bringing about a more desirable state of affairs than existing conditions promise for one of our minor industries." He sought cooperation between the planters in canning, warehousing, and shipping of canned pineapple. He felt that an organization could improve planning and help prevent overproduction, but grower James Dole strongly disagreed with the proposal. And, when the Pineapple Growers Association was organized three years later, its main goal was to promote Hawaiian pineapple on the North American Mainland.

Emmeluth also wanted the industry to hire an expert chemist to better control the quality of the canned product. Individual canners, still small operators, could not afford the cost of such an expert.

Englishman **E. W. Jordan** arrived in Honolulu in 1868, and was growing and selling Smooth Cayenne pineapple from his Nu'uanu Valley plantation by 1892. His brother, R. A. Jordan, had sent him three hundred plants from Queensland, Australia. Jordan was selling fruit for $1 apiece and plants for 25 cents. Thurston wrote that Jordan had twenty thousand plants of twenty-two varieties, which he had acquired from around the world, including Jamaica, Singapore, Bahamas, Samoa, Australia, and London. As with other growers, his shipments to the West Coast were making him money at the start and end of the fruiting season, but mid-season pineapple production was so high that it lost money. Jordan, one of the original stockholders in the Pearl City Fruit Company, was concerned that the increased plantings in Hawai'i would overwhelm the market, and he supported the idea of a cooperative cannery, which would preserve the surplus crop.

Jordan had reason to be concerned about the increase in the amount of pineapple being planted. He was in the forefront of the expansion of the industry. When his Nu'uanu property was filled up, he formed a partnership with Samuel Mills Damon and started another plantation at Moanalua, where he put in twelve thousand plants in 1892 and twenty-four thousand in 1893. Damon, head of the Bank of Bishop & Company, the former minister of finance under King Kalākaua and the director of several large sugar plantations, was likely the money behind Jordan's expansion.

In 1896, Jordan's brother in Australia bought an abandoned pineapple farm and shipped a million Smooth Cayenne plants to Hawai'i. The huge supply of the premier variety of pineapple gave the industry a tremendous boost. Jordan supplied other growers with plants. In 1903, he sold ninety-two thousand to Dole's Hawaiian Pineapple Company (Hapco).

Byron O. Clark, born May 24, 1855, in Iowa, had come across the American West in a covered wagon and worked on his family's California vineyard. He moved to Hawai'i in 1897, and in May 1898 was appointed the Hawaiian Republic's commissioner of agriculture and forestry. He recognized opportunity in the Land Act of 1895, which allowed the homesteading of government land. Since annexation by the United States of America was imminent, and there was a fear that annexation could repeal the law, he acted quickly to establish an interest in government land at Wahiawā. Clark invited a group of California farmers to move to Hawai'i and formed an association to buy the land. Kidwell, on going out of the pineapple business in 1898, had dumped plants into a ditch. Clark fished them out, planted them, and had his first harvest in 1900. He bottled some of the fruit in glass jars.

Among the California homesteaders was Leonard Kellogg, the brother of Clark's wife, Mary. The two of them and other homesteaders formed the Hawaiian Fruit and Plant Company, with Clark as its president. Clark entered into another pineapple business with A. W. Eames, one of the homesteaders, and they formed Tropic Fruit Company. Kellogg may have had a partnership interest, but apparently not a management interest in the firm. Tropic started off owning 5 acres and leasing 300 more from Dowsett Company Ltd,. at Wainaeuka, land adjoining the Wahiawā Tract to the southeast. The company expanded quickly. By 1906, Tropic had increased its ownership to 225 acres and leased 300, and by 1908, when it had merged with Hawaiian Fruit and Plant, it had 1,000 acres producing pineapple. Production went up with acreage: 75 tons in 1905, 300 tons in 1906, and 1,000 tons in 1907. Tropic canned some of its fruit in its own cannery.

Clark and Eames merged Tropic with Hawaiian Fruit and Plant in 1906, forming a company that was sometimes called the Consolidated Pineapple Company of Wahiawā and sometimes the Consolidated Wahiawā Company. Clark seems to have dropped out of the active pineapple scene about 1906, although he remained in Hawai'i for several more years. In 1911, the canning and growing operations were separated, with Eames getting control of the cannery, while other assets went to the Hawaiian Preserving Company, owned by both Hawai'i residents and the California Fruit Canners Association. The company was sold again in 1917 to California Packing Corporation, which would be known throughout Hawai'i as CPC.

Clark, during just a decade or so in the industry, had developed a number of innovations in the growing of pineapple. Earlier, the fruits had been planted in beds, but he initiated planting in long rows and cultivation by horse or mule. He invented one of the first effective disc harrows in the Islands, and experimented with removing the fruit's crown, which he believed robbed the fruit of weight. Today, chemical crown reduction is sometimes practiced for the same reason.

Clark also developed several techniques for handling pineapple after harvest. He designed crates with rounded corners to minimize fruit bruising and developed molds for glass jars specifically made for pineapple. Clark, with E. K. Ellisworth, invented a patented device for cutting pineapples into cubes and long rectangular pieces. The Tropic Fruit Company owned the patent. Clark also argued for cutting fruit lengthwise rather than horizontally, claiming this left the fruit with a better flavor.

While Clark left his mark on the pineapple industry, according to James Dole, he had left the islands by 1937.

W. B. Thomas was a California newspaperman who became one of the Wahiawā homesteaders. He would report that he came to Hawai'i for his health. His writing background helped provide a picture of those early days of the pineapple industry. He wrote a review of the Wahiawā Colony in the December 1900 *Paradise of the Pacific*, and published a number of other statements about the industry. It seems Thomas was well-respected by his fellow growers. James Dole wrote that Thomas was "a man of sound judgment and very straight thinking; a splendid man and one whose judgment in the pineapple business, as long as he lived, was valued by his associates and competitors in the business."

Thomas sold fresh fruit on the Mainland through the Pearson-Page Company of Portland. Once Dole built his Hapco cannery in 1902, Thomas delivered fruit there as well. He participated in the Tropic Fruit Company, and when it was sold, he started the Thomas Pineapple Company and built a cannery in Honolulu. Thomas had 600 acres in cultivation. He canned pineapple under the labels "Pride of Hawaii" and "Thomas' Best."

On his death in 1916, his son, Will P. Thomas, who had been manager of the Consolidated Pineapple Company, sold the entire Thomas pineapple operation to Libby, McNeill & Libby. The same year, Libby sold the cannery to L. C. Smith-Hiorth, who packed jams and "Pinector." Ultimately, Hawai'i Fruit Packers acquired the cannery, and ran it until it was destroyed in a fire.

Alfred W. Eames had the first choice of land among the Wahiawā colonists, and paid $4 an acre for his 100 acre lot. He started selling fresh fruit in 1900 and, in 1911, switched from fresh to canned fruit sales when he bought the Consolidated Pineapple Company cannery in Wahiawā. Eames, neighbor to James Dole, bought stock in Dole's Hapco in 1902, but the same year sold the stock and went into a separate venture with Byron Clark. After their Tropic Fruit Company merged to form Consolidated Pineapple, and once Consolidated Pineapple closed in 1911, Eames bought the cannery and started Hawaiian Islands Packing Company. He ran the company until his death in 1914. His son, Alfred Eames Jr., succeeded him as president, and in 1917 sold the cannery and other assets to CPC. Alfred Eames Jr. later served as president of CPC.

Leonard G. Kellogg, whose sister was married to Byron Clark, was an important figure in the early pineapple history of Hawai'i, but not much is known about him. He participated in the Tropic Fruit Company and in bringing water to the Wahiawā fields. James Dole called him "an important character in the pineapple industry; a man of immense energy and vitality who was very active in establishing the Wahiawā Water Company. Without him, it probably would not have been done."

JAMES D. DOLE

Jim Dole is probably the most important figure in the history and development of the Hawaiian pineapple industry. He was born in Boston, the son of a Congregational minister. Jim Dole's father was a cousin of Sanford Ballard Dole, the president of the Hawaiian Republic that was created after the overthrow of Queen Lili'uokalani and the first governor of the Territory of Hawai'i. Dole attended Harvard, and on graduation headed for Hawai'i. He had read Hawai'i Agriculture Commissioner, Joseph Marsden's 1893 bulletin, promoting the development of small coffee farms. The bulletin spoke of homestead lands that could be had for little cost, and talked of the wondrous possibilities of Hawaiian agriculture.

Dole arrived Nov. 16, 1899. He was twenty-two and he stayed with his father's powerful cousin. His first investment was a $1,500 stake in sugar companies. Then he learned that 61 acres of Wahiawā land was available. It was being given up by a discouraged homesteader of the Wahiawā Colony Tract. Dole consulted with Clark and Kellogg, then bought the land at government auction for $4,000. He moved to Wahiawā in August 1900, first living with the Clarks. He built a barn on his property and lived in it until he completed a one-room house.

Neighbors Clark and Eames harvested their first pineapples that summer.

With the removal of the 35 percent tariff on pineapple, the crop seemed to Dole a potentially profitable one. He had already identified Smooth Cayenne as the variety with a future. With a friend from New England named Fred Tracy and a horse, he got to work. He soon learned that weather was one of the banes of a farmer's existence, and that untrained carpenters build shaky houses. Dole later wrote, "We had always had trade-wind weather, and I had no idea there were such things as Kona storms . . . I well remember the first Kona storm we had at Wahiawā." Dole recounted:

> During the night it had begun to rain and finally began to blow, and it blew harder and harder until finally the house began to shake back and forth. If it went over it would go into the gulch, so I went out and slept in the barn. I went out there and laid down, but the storm got worse and worse and pretty soon I began to hear the sheets of iron that were blowing off the roof of Mr. Eames' house and we could hear Mr. Eames and Alfred trying to nail them on. I remember that Mrs. Gibson was over there with two or three babies and we wondered how they were getting along and we walked over in the mud. We found that the roof of their house had not been glued or nailed on solidly and so, as the wind blew, it lifted it up about a foot at a time, and up and down it went. We got some rope and lashed it down.

> We learned afterwards that Dr. Rhodes and his wife had about the same trouble, but in aggravated form. The middle of their roof went up and down about two feet. They finally got a rope around it but they had nothing to lash it to, and as Mrs. Rhodes was of considerably avoirdupois and Mr. Rhodes was rather light, they took a rope to bed with them and hung on to it all night.

Dole gathered investors mostly in Honolulu and in December 1901 capitalized his Hawaiian Pineapple Company (Hapco) with $16,240. But more money was needed for the perceived future of pineapple—canning. Dole went to the Mainland and spent a year there seeking funds. He picked up $13,000 in Boston and $15,000 in California. The California investors were J. H. Hunt and partner A. C. Baumgartner, who later became Hapco's sales manager. The cannery was completed in late 1903, but once the railroad was extended to Wahiawā and fruit could be shipped more easily, Hapco moved its canning operation to Iwilei, closer to the docks. The move came in 1906, the same year the American Can Company built a can manufacturing plant in Honolulu.

Hapco started out with 40 acres leased from Dole, 10 acres of which were actually in pineapple. But the firm expanded quickly. The company bought ninety-two thousand plants from Jordan for cash plus $2,100 in Hapco stock. The firm had an option to lease 300 acres from the Dowsett Company, whose manager, Walter F. Dillingham, Dole had known in New England. Hapco planted 30 acres in 1903, and took up 50 acres of its Dowsett option. The company also arranged for Dowsett to lease 400 acres to other growers, whose crops would be delivered to Dole's cannery.

The first year, 1903, Hapco's plant packed 70 tons of pineapple in 1,893 cases. In 1904 output more than quadrupled to 8,818 cases, growing to 25,022 cases in 1905, 31,934 cases in 1906, 108,600 cases in 1907, and 225,320 cases in 1908. Jim Dole's Hapco by this time was the biggest player in the industry, with more than half the Hawaiian canned production. The entire pineapple industry's output pack in 1908 was 400,000 cases. Hapco's production grew to 241,000 cases in 1909.

With all that production, Hawai'i needed promotion. Dole had been instrumental in forming the Hawaiian Pineapple

Growers' Association, which would continue under that name for three years and whose goal was the promotion of Hawaiian pineapple on the U.S. Mainland. All the territory's growers were members, with the exception of the Hawaiian Islands Packing Company and the Captain Cook Coffee Company.

The canneries of the 1900s could not have been as efficient as they were if not for Henry Ginaca, a mechanical draftsman for Honolulu Iron Works, who was hired by Dole in 1911. Ginaca designed a device that ever after would be known as "the Ginaca," or "the Ginaca machine." It was a machine that peeled, cored and removed the ends from a pineapple fruit, and it could cut fruits to size. Work previously done by hand could now be performed at a rate of eighty to one hundred pineapples a minute. Half a century later, the Ginaca was still the industry standard.

In 1918, Libby, McNeill & Libby proposed to Dole that Libby buy the island of Lāna'i, which seemed to be good pineapple land, and that Hapco sign a long-term lease on 5,000 acres there. The negotiations failed, but Dole remained interested in Lāna'i.

By 1922, Hapco had 48,000 tons produced from 9,400 acres, and Dole negotiated a nineteen-year renewable lease with Waialua Agricultural Company for 12,000 acres. He had already been leasing 3,676 acres from Waialua. Dole made a crucial deal for Waialua, which was partly owned by its agents, Castle & Cooke. For a one-third interest in Hapco, Hapco would get the Waialua land and $1.25 million in cash—it was the beginning of the association of Castle & Cooke with Dole and Hapco. Dole promptly took the cash from the Waialua deal and bought virtually the entire island of Lāna'i from Maui ranchers Frank and Harry Baldwin for $1.1 million. It was 1922 and with the Waialua land and Lāna'i, Hapco's farmable acreage had now increased to 40,000.

The next decade had its ups and downs. For Hapco, 1923 was an exceptionally profitable year. Dole, ever the promoter, looked for opportunities to keep Hawai'i in the minds of the American public. In 1927, he sponsored an airplane race from the Mainland to Hawai'i. It was an event that would haunt him for years afterward. Ten people involved in the race died. Several planes crashed during flight preparations or during the race takeoff, two were lost at sea, and two fliers died during rescue attempts.

Production for Hapco in 1931 reached 4.9 million cases, but the Depression had hit, and by the start of the 1932 harvest, Hapco still had 2.5 million cases of the previous year's crop unsold. Hapco was in deep financial trouble. Castle & Cooke stepped in, took control, and reorganized the company. Dole, aged fifty-six, was named chairman of the board of directors, but Castle & Cooke took over management of the company. Dole was frustrated by the change, but he did not have sufficient stock to prevent it. He took a vacation on the Mainland, and returned to find the company didn't seem to want him. "I found myself first without a desk room and then installed among the boxes and labels in the storeroom where I received friends of the company who could find me. Here I was almost completely ignored," he said. His salary had been cut from $50,000 to $15,000, but he had a stake in the company's profitability as well, so in the good years after the Depression, his pay was doubled. It remained at $30,000 for the rest of his life. The Depression's negative impact on pineapple sales waned within a couple of years. In 1934, sales were good. And by 1936, under Castle & Cooke's control, Hapco's $8.5 million debt had been transformed into a credit balance of $2 million.

Dole kept up his association with the company until 1948, when he was asked to give up his position. He did, and moved to San Francisco, where he ran a food machinery firm and acted occasionally as a pineapple consultant. He died in 1958 at age eighty.

OTHER EARLY PINEAPPLE INDUSTRY FIGURES

Charles Hansen, who encouraged Kidwell to grow pineapples.

W. E. Purvis, reported in some accounts to have imported the first Smooth Cayenne to Hawai'i from Kew Gardens in London.

Edward Lycan, said to have imported the first Smooth Cayenne when he sailed from Madeira in 1884.

Wahiawā homesteaders Dr. Emmit Rhodes and Thomas A. Gibson.

C. J. McCarthy, a former San Francisco fruit wholesaler who encouraged fresh pineapple sales in California and who, in 1892, was secretary of both the Woodlawn Fruit Company and the Pearl City Fruit Company.

C. D. Pringle grew pineapple in 1921 above Ka'ena Point. His effort to establish a cable to transport pineapple to the railhead failed, and he was forced to haul it over a rough, winding road.

Waka Dayashi, who grew pineapples above Ka'ena Point in 1921, was one of several growers who established plantings on the highlands overlooking O'ahu's westernmost point.

Sam P. Wood, who was a pineapple grower at North Kohala in 1908, sold his fruit to the Hilo Pineapple Company, and shipped it there by boat.

Dr. G. Trousseau, who planted two thousand plants of three or four varieties around Diamond Head in 1892. His plans for a major plantation never materialized.

John Ena paid 20 cents apiece for four thousand pineapple plants of seven varieties from Trinidad, Puerto Rico and Jamaica. In 1891 and 1892, Ena had twenty-three thousand plants growing.

George Burnside, who apparently gained experience growing pineapple in the Bahamas, was brought in as a pineapple expert for the Woodlawn Fruit Company about 1892.

Kahulila'au grew pineapple above the Nu'uanu Valley upper reservoir. He had five thousand plants imported from Florida and five thousand of the Wild Kailua variety. In 1892 he ran out of land for expansion.

Antone Rosa, at one time attorney general of the Hawaiian Kingdom, had one thousand plants, half imported and half native, growing near Kalihi. He reported in 1892 that he would be willing to expand his acreage if a cannery were built.

Lorrin A. Thurston, a partner with Kidwell and Emmeluth in the Hawaiian Fruit and Packing Company and also an early partner with Baldwin at Haleakalā Ranch Company on Maui, was chairman of the Committee on Fruit Culture about 1892. He was the author of much of the material written about the industry in those years.

J. L. Torbert and W. R. Sims had about one thousand plants imported from Florida growing at Pearl City in 1892. Torbert was auditor of the Pearl City Fruit Company and is believed to have been the first to experiment with recovering usable fiber from pineapple leaves.

J. P. Keppeler in 1893 experimented with irrigating pineapple fields. He pumped water from shallow wells near his fields in Wahiawā on O'ahu, and furrow-irrigated every ten days. While the process was an agricultural success, producing excellent fruits weighing 12 to 15 pounds, it wasn't cost-effective.

P. B. Camarinos had a Kalihi-kai plantation with fifty thousand imported plants. He had a San Francisco wholesale fruit company and was president of the Pearl City Fruit Company.

S. Kazanteno, during and after World War II, exported fresh pineapple through his company, Tropical Fruit Exchange of Hawai'i, Ltd. He also delivered fruit to Honolulu canneries. He died in 1958.

Ripe fruit in a pineapple field.

The Early
Pineapple Companies

F ollowing the efforts of pineapple pioneers is one thing, but following the lives of pineapple companies is another. The listing of early pineapple companies is no simple matter. Companies formed and failed, were bought and sold and altered. Company names changed as entities combined or split, investments were reapportioned, or operations shifted to subsidiaries. As in the formative years of other industries, many early business efforts failed. Assets were often utilized by later efforts. This chapter outlines in reference form the early pineapple companies in Hawai'i. The companies are presented in the general chronological order in which the businesses were formed and contain at least brief outlines of the scope of operations.

Woodlawn Fruit Company (1890–1898)

Woodlawn Fruit Company grew pineapples for the fresh fruit market from about 1890 to 1893. Woodlawn, with fields at Pearl City, was established as a corporation with P. B. Camarinos as president and C. J. McCarthy as secretary. It was capitalized with $30,000 and got started by importing fifty thousand plants from the Bahamas. The firm brought in Bahamas pineapple expert George Burnside. By 1898, the company was no longer in the listing of existing pineapple companies.

Pearl City Fruit Company (1890–1928)

Pearl City Fruit Company had fields at 'Ewa, near Pearl City. It was started when the O'ahu Railway extended a line to Pearl City in 1890, making it possible to get agricultural products to Honolulu. Inexpensive railway land was made available. Charles T. Wilder, W. C. Weedon, James Lyle, D. McLean and some other investors started the firm and arranged desirable terms with O'ahu Railway for land and shipping.

In 1891, the company planted fifteen thousand plants, all from imported stock, then twenty-five thousand plants in 1892, and was scheduled to put in fifty thousand in 1893. Because the U.S. tariff was limiting profitability, in 1898, Pearl City Fruit introduced some sugar among its pineapple acreage. The firm was considering abandoning pineapple altogether, but the tariff was lifted and conditions for pineapple suddenly looked bright again. The company's officers bought Kidwell's cannery in 1899, and started planting aggressively, picking up the Kidwell plants that Clark had discarded in ditches. At this time, Camarinos was president, J. L. Torbert auditor, and C. J. McCarthy secretary. James F. Morgan was another officer. Pearl City Fruit had the only operating cannery in 1901, but Dole would follow shortly. Theo H. Davies & Company. bought the company in 1906 and moved the cannery to Waiau. The company was gone by 1928.

Hawaiian Fruit and Packing Company (1892–1898)

Hawaiian Fruit and Packing Company, formed by John Kidwell, president, and John Emmeluth, treasurer, began with capital stock of $40,000. It started aggressively, planting one hundred thousand Queen and Smooth Cayenne plants on 145 'Ewa acres in 1893. They planned to plant two hundred thousand more plants in 1894. The firm bored an artesian well and established a pumping plant. Its Apoka'a cannery, west of Waipahu, produced its first pack in 1895 consisting of 486 cases of two dozen jars. S. J. Wilder shipped part of the production to California. The growers expected to expand production to five thousand cases the next year, but they were depending on an improvement in treaty relations between the United States and the Hawaiian Republic.

Emmeluth brought in a canning expert to improve the product, but the expert had no experience with pineapple and conducted extensive experimentation. One issue was how long to cook the fruit to properly preserve it without overdoing it. At the Apoka'a cannery, researchers tried 10 minutes, 20 minutes, and a half-hour. The eventual cannery practice was to cook the fruit for 14 minutes.

Henry May & Company was the initial distributor for Hawaiian Fruit and Packing, but Theo H. Davies & Company eventually controlled the local market by buying cases in quantity. Kidwell's interest turned to sugar as the tariff depressed the profitability of pineapple. In 1898, with Emmeluth probably already out of the picture, he sublet the pineapple lands to 'Ewa Sugar Company and closed the Apoka'a cannery. He formed the Apokaa Sugar Company, ironically, the same year the tariff was lifted. In all, Hawaiian Fruit and Packing had canned fourteen thousand cases and sold four hundred thousand fresh fruit.

Hawaiian Fruit and Plant Company (1899–1906)

Hawaiian Fruit and Plant Companywas established primarily to assist the California homesteaders at Wahiawā.

Byron O. Clark was the firm's leader, and with his brother-in-law, Leonard Kellogg, he held the major financial interest in the firm. The company initially sold fresh fruit, and later sold pineapple to Dole's cannery. Clark and Kellogg faded from active involvement after Clark started Tropic Fruit Company in 1902. In 1906, the Consolidated Pineapple Company of Wahiawā absorbed both Tropic Fruit and what was left of Hawaiian Fruit and Plant.

Tropic Fruit Company (1902–1906)

Tropic Fruit Company, with Clark as president and manager, devoted considerable effort to assisting needy homesteaders before the crops were harvested. The firm had an office at 72 King Street "where orders for fresh fruit to be shipped abroad may be filed and information generally may be had about their products." *The Pacific Commercial Advertiser* in 1906 credited Clark with having done "more than any[one] else to bring Hawaiian fruit to the attention of the world."

Up until the establishment of the American Can Company plant in Honolulu, when cans became the standard, Tropic Fruit canned much of its pack in glass jars. One of the Tropic Fruit products was "Sherbet pineapple," which was a pineapple sauce designed for use at soda fountains and in flavoring, desserts, and sherbet. There was strong demand for the product, whose label was copyrighted by Tropic Fruit.

The company started small. Clark and his family had limited funds, and arranged to exchange stock for a lease on land from the Dowsett Company. The firm took subscriptions for stock, under which buyers initially paid just 25 percent of the stock price. By 1906, the company had taken in 90 percent of its $100,000 capitalization. That year, Tropic Fruit and Hawaiian Fruit and Plant were combined into the

Consolidated Pineapple Company of Wahiawā, and each firm was valued at $100,000.

Haiku Fruit and Packing Company (1903–1935)

Haiku Fruit and Packing Company was started by the Baldwin family of Maui after thirteen years of independent pineapple production by Dwight D. Baldwin. He had started in 1890, and by 1900 his production had outstripped local demand. He tried West Coast sales, but the effort was not profitable. In 1903, his family started Haiku Fruit and Packing with $25,000 in initial capital. His brother Henry P. Baldwin was president and Dwight Baldwin served as vice president. D. B. Murdock was treasurer, H. A. Baldwin was a director, and W. A. Baldwin the manager.

Haiku Fruit and Packing built a cannery and a can-making plant in 1904 and 1905, and in that year shipped 14,000 cases—the first canned pineapple from Maui to go to California. Can labels carried the Hawaiian coat of arms, a pineapple, and the brand name, "Royal Hawaiian." Kidwell complained in 1905 that the product needed to be canned in pineapple juice for better flavor, and within a short time, the company switched to canning in a pineapple juice syrup.

Haiku Fruit and Packing and the Haiku Sugar Company were the biggest figures in the pineapple industry of that area but also did extensive business with independent farmers. Maui's independent planters had 150,000 plants in the ground. Haiku Fruit and Packing paid growers $25 per ton for No. 1 and No. 2 size fruit delivered to the cannery. Murdock, who lived at Pāʻia, Maui, wrote in 1906 that Maui's small growers had their fields primarily in the upper Makawao area: "Quite a number of pines are being raised by Portuguese farmers on the higher lands of Kaupakulua, at an elevation of about 1,400 feet, but the more serious efforts are being made at Ha'ikū, where the results continue to come up to, or even exceed, the early prognostications."

In 1911, when the Pukalani Dairy and Pineapple Company was sold, Haiku Fruit and Packing bought 350 acres of pineapple land.

In that same year, company president H. P. Baldwin died at the age of sixty-seven, and D. D. Baldwin died in 1912 at eighty. James Dole's Hapco bought a 51 percent interest in Haiku Fruit and Packing in 1912, held the control until 1918, and then sold to a group of Maui investors, headed by H. W. Rice, who combined Haiku Fruit and Packing with the island's first pineapple firm known as Maui Pineapple Company. Rice eventually sold his stock in the company to San Francisco financial agents Griffith Durney and Associates.

The Haiku Fruit and Packing canning plant remained operational, and in 1915, American Can Company built a can plant at Ha'ikū. In 1920 Charles Gay, who had bought the island of Lāna'i, arranged to plant pineapple there, for delivery to Ha'ikū for processing. By the next year he had 100 acres in pineapple. The company also took an interest in growing pineapple in the wet, windward portion of Maui and in 1922 bought the Kipahulu Sugar Company. It leased 200 acres of farm land in Mū'olea at Kīpahulu and started planting pineapple. Haiku's second cannery was built in 1924 at Hāna Bay. But the windward operation was not successful and was abandoned by 1927.

Moreover, in 1922, Hapco stepped in and took over agricultural operations on Lāna'i, and San Francisco financial agents Sutro & Company. got control of the company in 1926. Two years later the name was changed from Haiku Fruit and Packing to Haiku Pineapple Company.

Hapco returned to Maui in 1935 and bought Haʻikū Pineapple, which was succeeded by Island Pineapple Company. Hapco closed the Island Pineapple cannery in 1938 and sold its farm equipment, but kept the leases and arrangements with the Maui independent growers. In 1944, Hapco left Maui once and for all, selling all its remaining property there to T. Miyamoto.

Captain Cook Fruit Company (1906–1920)

Captain Cook Fruit Company established pineapple as an industry on Hawaiʻi's Big Island. W. W. Bruner, owner of Captain Cook Coffee Company, had apparently started growing pineapples on 5 to 6 acres at Nāpōʻopoʻo, south of Kona, in 1903. He formed Captain Cook Fruit in 1906. There is some difference of opinion about the site of the company's initial 30-acre fields. One source says it was above Nāpōʻopoʻo but another places it above Hoʻokena, 10 miles south, on land owned by W. R. Castle and later by the Magoon Estate. Thrum's 1909 Hawaiian Annual says Bruner started the firm on 30 acres of rocky but fertile soil, and put up three thousand cases of preserves in 1906. Later, 100 acres were planted above the cliffs between Nāpōʻopoʻo and the Kaʻawaloa monument to Captain Cook. Planting holes were prepared in the rocks with picks, and pineapples planted between the stones. The first plantings reportedly did well, but subsequent plantings did so poorly that Bruner brought a hardier variety in from Cuba , the Red Spanish pineapple, to replace the Sugar Loaf variety grown at Hoʻokena by J. B. and W. R. Castle. Bruner sold his cannery and coffee mill in 1911 to J. B. Castle. But the Castles were growing unhappy with pineapple. Bruner was interviewed in California in 1913, and reported that "rains, weeds and high cultivation costs made the Castles quit trying to grow pines on their Ho'okena properties." Castle brought in veteran Hawaiian pineapple cannery hand Robert "Pop" Lister, but ultimately, probably because of problems with growing the crop, sold the cannery. John Hind bought it and ran it for a few years. Hind dismissed the cannery engineer and ran it with a group of Japanese mechanics who had no canning experience. One entire season's pack, most likely the 1920 crop, was unsalable because of an odd taste. The problem is now believed to have been over-cooking. Hind closed the business after this experience.

Consolidated Pineapple Company of Wahiawa (1906–1911)

Consolidated Pineapple Company of Wahiawa, created by the merger of Tropic Fruit Company and Hawaiian Fruit and Plant Company, was often called the Wahiawa Consolidated Company. Initial capitalization of $200,000 — $100,000 from each company—was increased to $400,000 through stock sales. The firm's stock was listed on the exchange. *Mid-Pacific* magazine in 1911 reported that the company's cannery stood "in the midst of the biggest pineapple field in the world at Wahiawā, and here the fresh fruit may be picked every morning and canned in its own juice before night. This is the only company in Wahiawā that cans in the field." That was the year Consolidated was sold. Some of the assets went to Hawaiian Preserving Company, which sold the major interest to California Fruit Packers Association. The new owner sold to California Packing Corporation in 1917.

Hawaiian Islands Packing Company (1906–1917)

Hawaiian Islands Packing Company was officially organized in 1906. It was a continuation of Alfred W. Eames Sr.'s pineapple operation, which had its first harvest in 1900 after initial plantings in 1899. Some sources say Eames built a cannery in 1906, but there are indications he actually bought Consolidated's existing cannery.

Eames and Dole apparently did not get along well. Dole mentioned Eames only in passing in his later writings. And when Dole sought to rally the industry through the organization of the Hawaiian Pineapple Growers Association, Eames' firm, along with the Captain Cook Fruit Company, did not participate. When Eames died in 1914, his son, Alfred W. Eames Jr., took over. The younger Eames sold the cannery and other assets of Hawaiian Islands Packing Company to CPC in 1917.

Hilo Canning Company (1906–1921)

Hilo Canning Company has been known by several names, including Hilo Fruit Company, Hilo Fruit and Packing Company, and the Hilo Pineapple Company. (Another firm, started in 1921, was also called Hilo Pineapple Company.) Investors bought 4,000 shares at $10 apiece for an initial capitalization of $40,000. A cannery was built in Hilo in 1908. The company never had a plantation. It bought fruit from independent planters with patches around Hilo, and also brought in fruit by steamer from Kohala and Malama in Puna. Sam P. Wood in 1908 to 1909 grew pineapples in North Kohala that were sold to Hilo Canning. However, during the 1917 depression, the canning company found itself short of cash and unable to pay growers enough to keep them in the pineapple business. Hilo Canning shut down in 1921. Its buildings were sold to Hilo Iron Works.

Kauai Fruit and Land Company (1906–1929)

Kauai Fruit and Land Company started out as an adjunct to the McBryde Sugar Company. The sugar company, started in 1899, had only two profitable years between 1899 and 1909, and in 1909, the company ended its relations with agent Theo H. Davies & Company, and turned to Alexander & Baldwin, as agent and manager.

Kauai Fruit and Land was started in part as a way of keeping people in the area as independent farmers, so McBryde Sugar would have a source of employees. A small cannery was built at Lāwaʻi in 1907, and McBryde Sugar turned over 200 acres for planting. The sugar company provided water, power, and transportation facilities, and agreed to plant and maintain the fields at cost. McBryde agreed to buy all stock, but because of financial difficulties was relieved of this obligation. The pineapple company's initial capitalization was to have been $20,000, with 200 shares to be sold at $100 a piece, but only 150 shares were issued.

Walter McBryde, the son of the sugar company's founder, was named manager and was paid $100 monthly. The cannery's first pack was 2,575 cases, and it tripled in the first three years. Theo H. Davies & Company advanced the company money, and, in 1909, McBryde borrowed $50,000 from Kauai Railway Company to pay the agent back when Alexander & Baldwin took over. By 1928, Alexander and Baldwin owned all of Kauai Fruit and Land stock except for a few shares owned by Hawaiian Sugar Company. It bought these shares shortly thereafter and became sole owner.

In 1920, Kauai Fruit and Land farmed 1,100 acres in pineapple, and bought fruit from homesteaders who farmed 400 acres. The village of Lāwaʻi had forty or fifty homes, with a playground, a company-provided meeting hall, and a screened nursery "where the children of employed mothers are given attention during working hours." The company's name was changed in 1929 to Kauai Pineapple Company.

Thomas Pineapple Company (1906–1916)

Thomas Pineapple Company opened a cannery in Kalihi, O'ahu, in 1906, which was fed by W. B. Thomas' 600-acre Wahiawā plantation. It canned "Pride of Hawaii" and "Thomas' Best" brands. Thomas ran the plantation and cannery until his death in 1916, when his son, Will P. Thomas, sold the company to Libby, McNeill & Libby. Libby then turned the cannery over to L. C. Smith-Hiorth, who transferred it to Hawaiian Fruit Products Company, which ran it until it was destroyed by fire.

Koolau Fruit Company (1909–1910)

Koolau Fruit Company was established by J. B. Castle as a plantation on leased land at Kāne'ohe and He'eia. It had no cannery, and sold its fruit to Libby at its Kahalu'u cannery. At the same time, Castle and his brother were growing pineapple at Ho'okena on Hawai'i. Koolau Fruit Company and its leases were turned over to Hawaiian Pineapple Company, which continued to grow pineapple for sale to the Libby cannery. In 1916, Hapco sold the windward plantations to Libby, which grew pineapples on wet, windward O'ahu until 1927.

Hawaiian Cannery Company (1909–1910)

Hawaiian Cannery Company had a small cannery at 'Āhuimanu on windward O'ahu, which bought fruit grown by Ahuimanu Pineapple and Ranch Company, Ltd. In 1910 Libby bought both Hawaiian Cannery and Ahuimanu Pineapple and Ranch. The plantation had been owned by Honolulu businessman Fred W. MacFarlane, who became Libby's first general manager and kept the position until 1916. Fruit was processed at Libby's Kahalu'u cannery, at what was known as Libbyville. The cannery remained in production until 1922, when Libby dismantled the plant.

Haleakala Ranch Company/Haleakala Pineapple Company (1909?–1932),

Haleakala Ranch Company / Haleakala Pineapple Company owned by Henry P. and Samuel A. Baldwin, grew pineapples on the slopes of Maui's biggest mountain and delivered them to Haiku Fruit and Packing Company until 1923. That year, the pineapple plantings were expanded, and fruit was shipped to CPC's Honolulu cannery. Haleakala Ranch's pineapple operation was initially run as a department of the ranch, but in 1929 was converted to the Haleakala Pineapple Company, which merged in 1932 with Maui Agricultural Company's Grove Ranch to form the second Maui Pineapple Company.

The Maui Agricultural Company (1906–1932)

The Maui Agricultural Company was established in 1903 as a partnership of seven sugar companies. Grove Ranch was a member. Its first manager, David T. Fleming, was later the manager of Baldwin Packers. Grove Ranch started growing pineapple in 1906 and delivered the fruit to Haiku Fruit and Packing Company through 1923.

Henry Baldwin, manager of Maui Agricultural Company, suggested that Maui lands not suitable for sugar could be used for pineapple cultivation. The firm figured there was enough suitable land on the island to produce 1.5 million cases of pineapple a year. Baldwin, John Waterhouse, and W. Alexander considered building their own pineapple cannery, but ultimately negotiated an agreement with CPC to deliver pineapple to its cannery in Honolulu. Maui Agricultural had invested nearly $1 million in the pineapple business by 1929, and had a profit during that period of $754,295. In 1930, Maui Agricultural Company notified CPC that it would terminate its agreement to supply fruit to the Honolulu cannery, effective ten years after the agreement was signed.

The First Maui Pineapple Company (1910–1918)

The First Maui Pineapple Company was organized by Maui residents of Japanese ancestry with $20,000 in capital. Their cannery at Pa'uwela on east Maui canned fruit from contracted growers, and the first pack in 1910 was two thousand five hundred cases. The owners sold the company in 1918 to Haiku Fruit and Packing Company, which H. W. Rice and partners had just bought from Hapco.

Hawaiian Fruit Products Company (1918–1932)

Hawaiian Fruit Products Companystarted as a firm for preserving guava and other Hawai'i-grown fruit. F. W. Klebahn Sr. opened the company with a Mr. Stange as manager. Klebahn bought 2.5 acres of land in Kalihi near Waiakamilo Road and built a cannery at the location where a Libby plant would later be located. Some of the first pineapple delivered to Hawaiian Fruit Products was from independent Moloka'i growers at Kala'e, and from Waialua to Hālawa on the island's east end. The growers were generally undercapitalized, had insufficient knowledge about soil preparation, and were faced with high costs of hauling their fruits to the wharf at Kamalō, consequently most failed.

Early on, Hawaiian Fruit Products financed fields on the Moloka'i lands of the Brown Estate at what is now Pu'u o Hoku Ranch, but by 1920, those contracts had gone to CPC and Libby, for delivery to their Honolulu canneries. In 1920 Manager

Stange leased land in 'Aiea Heights, O'ahu, and in other locations. He contracted with various independent growers for the delivery of fruit to the cannery. Klebahn had been on the Mainland for health reasons in 1920. When he returned in 1921, the company was shut down. Hawaiian Fruit Products' assets were sold in 1922 to a local group called Honolulu Fruit Company headed by C. K. Ai. The group improved the cannery. In 1932, when Libby bought Honolulu Fruit Company's assets, it closed and dismantled the canning facility.

Hawaiian Preserving Company (1911–1918)

Hawaiian Preserving Company was incorporated by a group of Hawai'i residents in January 1911 and bought some assets of the Consolidated Pineapple Company of Wahiawā. The majority of Hawaiian Preserving's stock was sold soon after its formation to California Fruit Canners Association. The company built a cannery and bought land in Iwilei in 1911. CPC bought the company in 1917 and closed it the next year.

Ka-la Pineapple Company Ltd. (1919–1931)

Ka-la Pineapple Company Ltd. took over the Kāne'ohe cannery of a preserve-making firm, Hawaiian Fruit Canning Company. Ka-la bought fruit from growers and also leased 500 acres scattered around O'ahu for pine production. It ran into financial trouble in the late 1920s. A Honolulu hotelier named Yamashiro then took it over and ran it for two years. The aged equipment was sold and the building torn down in 1930 or 1931.

Honolulu Fruit Company (1922–1932)

Honolulu Fruit Company was established by local residents who had bought the assets of Honolulu Fruit Products

Company. Libby acquired its assets and dismantled its cannery in 1932.

Pauwela Pineapple Company (1919–1926)

In 1920, Pauwela Pineapple Company built a concrete pineapple cannery at Kuiaha near Pa'uwela in Maui's Ha'ikū district, just east of Haiku Fruit and Packing Company's cannery. Pauwela's president and manager was Ching Hing, and its field superintendent was J. A. Templeton. The Newhall-Haslett group of California bought into the firm in late 1920. S. M. Haslett became president and A. Newhall, secretary. The two remained directors of the firm until its sale to Libby in 1926, but in 1922, the San Jose, California, canning firm of Case & Richmond assumed management and control of the firm. Pauwela leased land from Marshall Ranch at Kahakuloa on west Maui and started growing pineapples in 1922. Libby bought a three-year lease and purchase option in 1926 and in 1928 exercised its option, buying all assets, including the cannery. Pa'uwela became the center of Libby's Maui activities.

Kohala Pineapple Company (1919–1931)

Kohala Pineapple Company was started in 1919 by the Pratt-Low Preserving Company of Santa Clara, California with $100,000 in capital. Officers included J. F. Wood as president, Sam P. Wood, who had grown pineapples in North Kohala as early as 1908, as vice-president, and Dexter Frazer, later Hapco manager on Lāna'i, as plantation manager. Frazer ran the plantation from 1919 to 1922. The company built a cannery four miles northeast of the port of Māhukona on the Big Island's Kohala Coast. By 1921 the firm owned or leased 6,045 acres. The first pack in 1921 included fruit shipped from 'Ōla'a and Puna, but most of the fruit was grown by the company on its own plantation. The factory featured two Ginaca machines and one box-making unit. The machinery was sold in 1939 to Hawaiian Fruit Packers on Kaua'i. The company's rolling stock included a 45-horsepower Holt tractor and two Cleveland tractors, a 5-ton Pierce Arrow, a 1-ton Ford truck, and two Ford cars. In 1931 Pratt-Low sent its own manager to Hawai'i to close the company.

Hawaii Fruit Packers Ltd., Honolulu, (1920–1924?)

Hawaii Fruit Packers Ltd., Honolulu, acquired the Thomas Pineapple Company cannery from L. C. Smith-Hiorth, who had gotten it from Libby, which bought Thomas Pineapple in 1916. Smith-Hiorth became a director of Hawaii Fruit Packers. The cannery had a fifty thousand-case capacity and fruit came by truck and rail from all over O'ahu. A San Francisco broker sold all the canned pineapple. The broker held a chattel mortgage on the fruit contracts the company held with its growers. The cannery packed 7,453 cases in 1920, half under Hawaii Fruit Packers' own label and half under a private label. The pack in 1921 was up to 20,644 cases, reached 23,542 in 1922, and 40,806 in 1923. The cannery burned down, probably in 1924, since there are no records of a pack after 1923, and the company closed.

Honolulu Canning Company (1920–1926)

Honolulu Canning Company was organized by Chinese investors in Honolulu, and started under general manager A. B. Lau, who had worked with Hapco from 1912 to 1920. Honolulu Canning never built a cannery, though it bought a seven-acre cannery site in Kalihi. The cannery site was later bought by the Territory of Hawai'i, and became the site of Pu'uhale School. The company leased 100 acres at Kualoa, 125 at Wailupe, and 80 at Waimea, and contracted with Libby to have fruit grown at these locations. When the company stopped operating in 1926, Libby bought most of the assets.

Hilo Pineapple Company (1921–1926)

Hilo Pineapple Company was the second attempt at developing a cannery operation at Hilo. The first, Hilo Canning Company, had sometimes been referred to as Hilo Pineapple Company. When Hilo Canning closed, a group of Hilo residents formed Hilo Pineapple Company, and leased 400 acres at Honoka'a. Libby was contracted to farm the land, and the fruit was shipped to Libby's Honolulu cannery. The company closed in 1926.

Keaau Agricultural Company (1921–1924)

Keaau Agricultural Company was started on high elevation land near Kea'au on Hawai'i. Partners J. S. "Jack" Mackenzie and A. J. Alexander dug wells, cleared and fenced plantation land and built a labor camp and houses for supervisors. They acquired planting material from the Pearl City Fruit Company, which was to buy the fruit. Oahu Railway and Land Company ran a railway line to Kea'au in 1922, the year the first 46 acre crop was harvested. But severe weather doomed the business. In June 1924, a storm washed out the plants and destroyed the labor camp. Mackenzie's house was moved 19 feet off its foundation, and its roof, covered in galvanized metal, was found 3 miles from the site. The company closed as a result of the devastation.

Haleakala Pineapple Company (1923, 1929–1932)

Haleakala Pineapple Company was developed on land that had been the ranch of Charles H. Alexander, brother of

Alexander & Baldwin founder Samuel T. Alexander. On Charles Alexander's death in 1885, E. H. Bailey and L. A. Thurston bought the ranch, and in 1888, H. P. Baldwin bought into it. Before long, Baldwin and Thurston owned 5,950 acres, essentially all the land below an extension to the Hāmākua Ditch. Samuel A. Baldwin began buying into Haleakalā Ranch Company in 1915, and, ultimately, he and H. P. Baldwin were the sole owners.

Haleakala Ranch grew a limited amount of pineapple for sale to Haiku Fruit and Packing Company. The firm expanded its operation and in 1923, along with Maui Agricultural Company, contracted with CPC to ship the fruit for ten years to CPC's Honolulu cannery, subject to a three-year notice of cancellation. The pineapple operation ran from 1923 to 1929 as the Haleakala Ranch Company's Pineapple Division, but in 1929, the Haleakala Pineapple Company was established as a separate company. In 1932, the company merged with the Grove Ranch Department of the Maui Agricultural Company, forming the second Maui Pineapple Company.

Glace Fruit Company (1924–1925)
Glace Fruit Company packed 17,539 cases in 1924 and 12,462 cases in 1925, but little else is recorded about this firm.

Honolulu Packing Company (1926–1928)
Honolulu Packing Company produced 16,200 cases in 1926, 10,136 in 1927, and 21,000 cases in 1928, but like Glace Fruit, little else is recorded.

Island Pineapple Company (1935–1938)
Island Pineapple Company was the name Hapco gave Haiku Pineapple Company when it bought the Maui company

in 1935. Hapco closed its cannery three years later and removed farm equipment, but honored its contracts with growers. All remaining buildings, some land, and a water supply system were sold in 1944 to T. Miyamoto, and the cannery water supply system was turned over to Maui County.

Kohala Sugar Company (in pineapple 1950–1952)

Kohala Sugar Company planted 400 acres in pineapple in late 1950, using planting material from Moloka'i and Maui. The company was already having trouble surviving as a sugar grower on the wet windward slopes of the Big Island, and was searching for alternate crops. The firm invested $250,000 in what would be an expensive experiment. The company harvested its first and only crop in 1952 and sold the fruit to Hapco, then shut down its pineapple venture, citing a poor economic climate for pineapple. The company ploughed under most of the crop, although it kept a small amount of pineapple to provide planting material in case it decided to reenter the business.

Entertainer Arthur Godfrey (right) celebrates Hawaiian statehood
with Libby-Hawai'i vice president L. Verne Hass.

CHAPTER FOUR

The Ten Postwar Companies

A fter the close of World War II, just eleven pineapple companies operated in Hawai'i. One of these was Kohala
Sugar Company's short experimental effort (see page
49). Kohala and the Pacific Pineapple Company of Moloka'i, started after the war but the others had been opened before the war
started. The three major firms were Dole, Libby, and Del Monte,
each with multi-island operations. Kaua'i-only companies included Kaua'i Pineapple Company, Hawaiian Canneries, Hawaiian
Fruit Packers, and Grove Farm. On Maui were Maui Pineapple
Company and Baldwin Packers. And Moloka'i's only operation
that did not also operate elsewhere was Pacific Pineapple.

Three of the Kaua'i companies closed in the 1960s, and
the remaining Hawaiian Fruit Packers lasted for a short time
into the next decade. Baldwin Packers on Maui merged into
Maui Pineapple, and Libby sold out to Dole in 1970. By 1992,
Dole and Del Monte were no longer canning but producing
only fresh fruit. Maui Pineapple Company was the only firm in
Hawai'i that was still a full cannery operation thereafter—it
had been canning pineapple since 1932. Dole's canning history
had lasted eighty-eight years, from 1902 to 1990. Del Monte
had canned for seventy-three years, from 1917 to 1990. And
Libby canned for sixty-one years, from 1909 to 1970.

DOLE AND THE HAWAIIAN PINEAPPLE COMPANY (1901–Present)

Jim Dole arrived in Hawai'i a recent Harvard graduate in 1899. His uncle was Sanford Dole, president of the new Republic of Hawai'i, and one of the men who had participated in the overthrow of Queen Lili'uokalani in 1893. He quickly set about getting into the pineapple business. He started Hawaiian Pineapple Company (Hapco) with 60 acres purchased from a Wahiawā homesteader, along with two horses, a harrow, and a plow. Dole tried to raise $20,000 in capital for the business, but ran into difficulty. Pineapple had already been around for many years, and many Honolulu residents were skeptical of the crop's future. Among the companies that turned him down was Castle & Cooke, which would ultimately run Dole's company. The *Advertiser* wrote that "If pineapple paid, the vacant lots near town would be covered with them." So Dole went to the Mainland for help, where he picked up $14,000 in Boston and more in California. Major backers included Joe Hunt who would form Hunt Foods, and Blumlein and Sussman who would form S&W.

Dole's cannery went up at Wahiawā in 1903. It was an all-purpose structure covering 3,900 square feet, with an attached barn for six horses, along with living quarters for twelve workers. The construction cost, including cannery equipment, was $13,100. The 1903 pack was 1,893 cases, 8,810 in 1904, and in 1905 it was 25,000 cases. In 1907, once a rail connection between Honolulu and Wahiawā was complete, Dole moved the cannery to Honolulu.

In the same year, a depressed economy on the Mainland cut into Hawai'i pineapple sales, and growers renewed discussions of an organized, cooperative pineapple industry that would market itself more effectively. Dole stepped in and helped organize the Association of Hawaiian Pineapple Growers. All the companies but Hawaiian Island Packing and Captain Cook Coffee Company joined. The association promoted Hawaiian pineapple in Mainland magazines.

In 1907 Dole began expanding onto land leased from Waialua Agricultural Company, which made acreage not suitable for sugar production available to pineapple growers. By 1916, he was leasing 3,676 acres from Waialua. In 1911, Dole's Hapco bought Koʻolau Fruit Company's Windward Oʻahu leases in Kāneʻohe and Heʻeia, which delivered fruit to the Libby cannery at ʻĀhuimanu, or "Libbyville."

In 1922, Dole went back to Waialua and arranged a seventeen-year lease of 12,000 acres of non-sugar land and got Waialua to invest in Hapco. He gave Waialua a one-third interest in Hapco in return for the lease and $1.25 million in cash. Castle & Cooke owned 20 percent of Waialua and was its agent and principal stockholder. The Waialua-Hapco arrangement linked Castle & Cooke to Hapco for the first time. Soon, Castle & Cooke was handling Hapco's insurance and freight business. In 1922, the company shipped 790,000 cases for Dole's firm.

Dole and Libby discussed operations on the island of Lānaʻi as early as 1918. Libby proposed to buy the island if Hapco would take a long-term lease on 5,000 acres. The negotiations weren't concluded, but Dole had set his sights on the island.

In 1920, Charles Gay's Lanai Land and Development Company had started shipping pineapple to Maui's Haiku Fruit and Packing Company. Dole watched with interest, and in 1922, he bought the island from Frank and Harry Baldwin who had owned it since 1917. Flush with the cash from its deal with Waialua, Hapco paid $1.1 million, most of the Waialua money, for this purchase.

Pineapple can label.

Pineapple can label.

Dole's Honolulu water tank in the shape of a pineapple.

In 1930, Hapco made nearly $1 million, but the oncoming depression quickly began battering the company. Not yet aware of the magnitude of the national economic collapse, Dole was still expanding. Already owing banks $3.5 million, he floated debentures to raise another $5 million for plant expansion. The 1931 earnings were down $120,372 to $840,370. The company cut salaries and pensions in 1932. Hapco had huge inventories of canned fruit, and had 230 million plants in the ground, all of them ready to bear fruit during the next eighteen months. Dole had developed processes to produce an improved pineapple juice, but he couldn't find the time or money to promote the product. He held the line on his prices, and lost market share. His creditors grew anxious.

Castle & Cooke had not been hit too hard by the Depression, but it worried about Waialua's interest in Hapco. Mainland banks expressed concern. Several large companies, including General Foods, began eyeing Hapco as a potential takeover target. Castle & Cooke saw this, and decided to find a way to keep Hapco Hawaiian. In 1932 Hapco was reorganized. Castle & Cooke assumed a 21 percent investment and Waialua had 37 percent. So between them, they owned more than half. Dole was named chairman of the board, but management was controlled by Castle & Cooke. The pineapple business recovered from the Depression, and by 1936 had turned its $8.5 million debt into a $2 million credit balance.

In 1948, Dole was asked to give up the chairman's post and end his relationship with the company. He did and moved to the Mainland, where he died at age eighty in 1958. Three years later, Castle & Cooke merged Hapco and Columbia River Packers into the parent company, and announced the creation of two new wholly-owned subsidiaries: Dole Pineapple Company and Bumble Bee Seafoods, along with Oceanic

Properties, which would manage Castle & Cooke's lands. Dole Pineapple would be renamed Dole Foods Company. While Jim Dole's name had been actively used in advertising his company's pineapple, it was only after his death that the company got his name.

The Hawaiian pineapple industry recognized the problems of high costs in Hawai'i and competition with cheap foreign imports, and in the early 1960s began moving abroad itself. In 1963, Dole formed Dole Philippines, nicknamed Dolefil, for the purpose of farming 18,000 acres 650 miles south of Manila, on the west coast of Mindanao. In 1964, Castle & Cooke bought 55 percent of Standard Fruit and Steamship Company of New Orleans. By 1968, it had full control of the company, a major banana grower with interests in Honduras, Costa Rica, and Nicaragua's Pacific coast. Ultimately, it would move across the Pacific to grow bananas in Mindanao for the Japan market. Dole was consolidated with Castle & Cooke, and then placed under the control of the Standard Fruit banana group in 1972.

Dole started a pineapple plantation and cannery in Thailand in 1974, as well as a fresh-fruit pineapple plantation in Honduras. It had acquired Libby's Hawaiian operations in 1970, including the firm's 12,500 acres on Moloka'i and the Libby cannery at Kalihi on O'ahu. But two years later, Dole shut down the cannery, and began winding down the plantation, whose closing was complete in 1975.

Dole had been shipping fresh pineapple from Hawai'i to the West Coast in refrigerated containers since the early 1960s, and air-freighting some fruit to eastern markets. The Wahiawā plantation's production was increasingly diverted to the fresh-fruit market as canned Hawai'i pineapple profits were reduced. In 1975, Donald Kirchoff, a former Standard

Fruit president, was named to replace Malcolm MacNaughton as president of Castle & Cooke. He was familiar with the fresh-fruit market and had confidence in fresh pineapple's future. He said per capita consumption of pineapple in 1975 was 0.8 pounds and could be increased.

Five years later, in 1980, Castle & Cooke was in financial trouble, blaming competition and bad weather. The problems continued, and the firm lost tens of millions of dollars annually during the first half of the 1980s. The balance book in 1985 showed equity of $295 million and debts of $491 million. The company was unable to make payments on its debts. It was saved by aggressive businessman David Murdock, who merged Castle & Cooke into his New York equipment leasing company, Flexi-Van. The latter firm was spun off in 1987, and Murdock was left Castle & Cooke's largest stockholder, with 25 percent of outstanding shares.

Dole remained the biggest pineapple producer in the world, but its pineapple operations in Hawai'i began shrinking. The Lāna'i plantation was cut from 3,200 acres to 750 acres in 1981, and was closed in 1992. Murdock had plans to develop the island of Lāna'i into a high-end resort. The Iwilei cannery stopped canning pineapple in 1992 and closed the next year. The Wahiawā fields covered 7,700 acres, and half the production had been going to the cannery. Once it closed, the frozen pineapple concentrate function was moved from Iwilei to a site near Wahiawā, and the plantation emphasized fresh-fruit production.

THE (SECOND) MAUI PINEAPPLE COMPANY (MAUI LAND AND PINE) (1932–Present)

Maui Pine, as it is commonly called, resulted from the 1932 merger of the Haleakala Pineapple Company, previously Haleakala Ranch's Pineapple Department, with the Pineapple Division of the Maui Agricultural Company. Haleakala held 5,089 shares and Maui Agricultural 4,911 shares. It had capitalization of $1 million and a surplus of $1.05 million. That year the companies cancelled their agreements to deliver fruit to CPC's cannery and exercised an option to buy CPC's Kahului cannery. The purchase was financed by Alexander & Baldwin, which became agent and factor for the new firm in January 1934. The new company's headquarters were established at Hāli'imaile, in the midst of Maui's pineapple country. The first manager was J. Walter Cameron, the former manager of Haleakala Pineapple, who was related by marriage to the Baldwins of Alexander & Baldwin.

The company started in the middle of the Great Depression, but in its favor were good climate, soil, and water, a downhill run from the pineapple fields to the cannery, and a cannery near the harbor. All that and good management helped the company pay off its outstanding debt in less than five years. It paid its first dividend in 1937. Another pineapple operation, Baldwin Packers, closed its Lahaina cannery in 1962 and merged with Maui Pine. Its pineapples were trucked from the slopes of West Maui around to the Kahului cannery. In 1968 Alexander & Baldwin exchanged stock with the Cameron family, and gave up all interest in Maui Pine, which was renamed Maui Land and Pineapple Company to reflect an interest in managing extensive lands, not all of which were in pineapple. Some of the pineapple lands were made available for other uses, and to regain lost fruit volume, it arranged with C. Brewer's Wailuku Agribusiness in 1986 to grow pineapple, ultimately on 2,000 acres of former sugar land. The crop was delivered to the Maui Land and Pine cannery.

The company sold no pineapple under its own name. Instead, it sold its entire pack to private labels. While Maui Land and Pine was buffered somewhat from the direct effects of foreign competition by this arrangement, times have been hard during the past decade. Maui Land and Pine has been losing money on pineapple in recent years. The company blames this in part on the dumping of cheap foreign canned pineapple on U.S. markets.

DEL MONTE (CALIFORNIA PACKING CORPORATION) (1917–Present)

CPC, sometimes called Calpack or Calpac, as its name implies, was a California canning firm. It was the third large corporation to enter the Hawaiian pineapple scene. In 1917 it acquired interests with early histories steeped deep in the Hawaiian pineapple history.

In 1906 Clark's Tropic Fruit Company and the Wahiawa homesteaders' Hawaiian Fruit and Plant Company merged to form the Consolidated Pineapple Company of Wahiawa. Clark, Eames, Thomas, and Kellogg were all involved. The cannery was sold in 1911 to Eames' Hawaiian Islands Packing Company. The other assets were sold to the Hawaiian Preserving Company, a new firm whose main stockholder was California Fruit Canners Association. Hawaiian Preserving bought land in Iwilei on O'ahu in 1911 but was dissolved in 1917, when CPC bought it. CPC also picked up Hawaiian Islands

Packing from Alfred Eames Jr., who had taken over the firm on his father's death in 1914. The younger Eames became CPC's manager in Hawai'i, and was president of CPC from 1940 until his death in 1948. CPC expanded its O'ahu plantings to include fields in Wahiawā, Kunia, Kahuku and Sanatarium Flats.

Hawaiian Fruit Products Company had financed pineapple plantings on Brown Estate lands near Hālawa on Moloka'i, now a part of Pu'u o Hoku Ranch. The fruit was shipped to the Kalihi cannery. In 1920, the Moloka'i fruit contracts were transfered—part to Libby and part to CPC, for delivery to their Honolulu canneries. The shipments continued into 1925.

The Grove Ranch of Maui Agricultural Company and Haleakala Ranch's pineapple operation arranged a 1923 agreement with CPC. Both had been delivering fruit to Haiku Fruit and Packing Company. The CPC agreement was a ten-year deal, with a requirement of a three-year notice of cancellation by either party. Grove would plant 500 to 600 acres per year and Haleakala 150 to 200 acres. The Maui companies would deliver the fruit to the dock on Maui, and CPC would barge, can, and sell it. Each firm would first be repaid their costs, and profits would be split 55 percent to the grower and 45 percent to CPC. In 1926 CPC built the Kahului cannery, with the agreement that if the contract between the canner and the growers was terminated, the growers would buy the cannery at its book value. In 1932, the two growers merged, and bought out CPC, ending that firm's involvement with Maui.

CPC had started a plantation at Kualapu'u on central Moloka'i in 1927, four years after Libby's start on west Moloka'i. The company leased land from Moloka'i Ranch and from Hawaiian homesteaders at Ho'olehua. The crop was trucked to Kaunakakai Wharf, a four- to five-mile distance, for shipment by barge to Kapālama Basin on O'ahu, for canning.

CPC also briefly grew pineapple on the Big Island of Hawai'i, but areas suited for pineapple growing were difficult to access, and the company dropped the operation after a short time.

CPC sold much of its product under the name Del Monte, and eventually changed its own name to that of the brand. Del Monte started a plantation on the island of Mindanao in the Philippines in 1926, during the Hawai'i industry's battle with the mealy bug. The Philippines Packing Corporation had many early problems, but became extremely successful, and today it is the largest pineapple operation in the world. The company's Kunia pineapple fields were converted to a profitable fresh-fruit operation, with a packing house on the plantation and a juice concentrate plant that was used to process fruit not suitable for sale in the fresh market.

In the 1970s, the R. J. Reynolds Tobacco Company bought the firm, and Del Monte's Hawai'i cannery was closed in 1983. However, despite repeated indications it was closing, Del Monte kept its Moloka'i plantation going through 1988. The eventual closure was the end of pineapple on Moloka'i. Del Monte sold its fresh-fruit operation and canning enterprises to different entities. The company's fresh-fruit operations are now managed from Miami, Florida, though still under the Del Monte name. Internationally, the company is owned by United Kingdom interests, Del Monte Royal Foods Ltd.

LIBBY, McNEILL & LIBBY (1909–1970)

This major Hawai'i pineapple firm started out as Libby, McNeill & Libby of Honolulu Ltd., a subsidiary of L.,M.,L., a Maine corporation headquartered in Chicago. In 1930 the subsidiary's assets were transferred to the parent company.

Night harvesting at Waipiʻo, Oʻahu, in 1950. In the summer, when the fruit was ripe, crews worked around the clock to harvest and get the crop to the canning plant.

Libby's first general manager for windward Oʻahu, Fred McFarlane, stands among ripe fruit in Waipiʻo.

Libby of Honolulu took off aggressively, acquiring leases and land in several locations and expanding dramatically after its June 14, 1909, incorporation. It was packing more than a million cases of pineapple by 1919, and eventually had plantations on three islands and canneries on two of them.

Libby on Windward O'ahu.

In 1909, the company bought Honolulu businessman Fred W. MacFarlane's Ahuimanu Ranch and Pineapple Company and the Hawaiian Cannery Company, which had a small plant at 'Āhuimanu, five miles north of Kāne'ohe. The next year, Libby built its own pineapple cannery at Kahalu'u. It grew some pineapple on its own, but also bought fruit from a number of independent growers who delivered it to the cannery. Fred MacFarlane was Libby's Hawai'i general manager from 1909 to 1916, and his son Walter was general plantation manager from 1914 to 1917.

In 1912, Libby bought 600 acres of leaseholds in Waiāhole and Waikāne. The same year, it opened its Honolulu office on lower Fort Street. More leased land was acquired in the Kāne'ohe–He'eia area in 1914, and in 1917, Libby obtained 600 acres of leasehold land from the He'eia Agricultural Company and 500 acres on northern Windward O'ahu from Hapco's Ko'olau Fruit Company. In addition, the Kāne'ohe Ranch Company leased Libby 1,200 acres around Kāne'ohe and Kailua in 1918, and the next year Libby subleased some of its lands to growers who delivered fruit to the cannery.

When Hawai'i men began shipping out to serve in World War I, Libby found it had lost a hundred workers to the draft. The company arranged to move the entire Korean school from Honolulu to Kahalu'u so the youngsters could work in the cannery during the pineapple season. Libby provided school facilities and living quarters.

Libby's first canning plant was built in 1910 at the mouth of 'Āhuimanu Stream in Kahalu'u. The post office in the area was called Libbyville. Note Mokoli'i, or Chinaman's Hat, in the background.

In 1918 Kaneohe Ranch Company leased Libby 1,200 acres around Kāne'ohe and Kailua, and the next year Libby sub-leased some of its lands to growers who delivered fruit to the cannery. The firm now controlled 5,000 acres that were in pineapple cultivation on Windward O'ahu. The area from below the Pali, stretching from Ka'a'awa to Kailua was virtually all in pineapple. The company's economic role in the area was so great that when a post office was started at the Kahalu'u cannery, it was called Libbyville. But the company was learning that pineapple didn't thrive in the wet, cloudy weather of Windward O'ahu. Its fields were smaller than needed for efficient operations, yields were lower, wilt was more prevalent, and growing costs were generally higher. In 1922 it dismantled the cannery. The Libbyville post office was closed and the company moved its operations to the other side of the Ko'olaus, where weather was better. Individual windward growers continued delivering fruit to Libby at its new Kalihi cannery until 1925.

High school students armed with hoes march through Oʻahu pineapple fields in 1944. Students were often hired by plantations for fieldwork during the summer months.

Libby in Central Oʻahu.

A number of individual growers at Waipiʻo, Halemano, and Kahuku contracted in 1914 to provide pineapple to Libby. The company leased 200 acres at Halemano and built its new cannery on 11 acres at Kalihi.

The company started its Waipiʻo plantation in 1915, after buying out the crops and leases of a number of growers and leasing 100 acres from the John ʻĪʻī estate at Waipiʻo. It leased 300 acres at Leilehua near Wahiawā in 1916 and bought 1,800 acres, half of which was arable, at Pūpūkea from Haley and other homesteaders.

In 1917 Libby took over the holdings of a group of growers who operated as the Waipiʻo Pine Company, including another 400 acres of John ʻĪʻī estate property. The firm also bought the Thomas Pineapple Company, which had a few hundred acres at Pomaho north of Wahiawā and Kunia to the south of Wahiawā. Will P. Thomas, the son of founder

Interior view of the Libby pineapple cannery
in Kalihi showing several packing "lines."

W.B. Thomas, sold the land to Libby, while the small Thomas cannery he sold to L. C. Smith-Hiorth. Hawai'i Fruit Packers later acquired it, and it was eventually destroyed by fire. By 1918, with the acquisition of more individual growers' land, the Libby Waipi'o plantation had 1,500 acres. The next year it added 319 acres at Kupehau south of Kunia, and 200 acres at Pomaho.

Libby employee Dan Derby grew pineapple for five years, starting in 1921, on the Big Island, shipping the fruit to the Kalihi cannery. The Hilo Pineapple Company had been organized at Honoka'a but never built a cannery. Their fruit also went to Kalihi cannery by inter-island steamer.

Libby picked up 466 acres near Kunia in 1921. In 1923, it added 300 acres of leased land at Pearl City, 100 acres at Kupehau, and 188 acres at Leilehua. In 1928, Libby leased 500 acres of old Pearl City Fruit Company land near Wahiawā. This ended expansion on O'ahu. Libby had started its new Moloka'i plantation in 1923 and was expanding rapidly there after shipping its first fruit to the Kalihi cannery in 1925.

The Waipi'o plantation continued for another three decades before closing in 1960. The Kalihi cannery, which could process 125,000 cases a day, was sold to Dole with the rest of Libby's assets when the company left Hawai'i. Dole ran the plant during the 1970 and 1971 seasons, then closed and dismantled it.

Libby on Moloka'i.

The island of Moloka'i, visible as a misty figure 26 miles to the east of O'ahu, had just six hundred to seven hundred residents in 1922. There was one small town at Kaunakakai, where there was also a wharf. The entire western side of the island was in pasture. It was notably dry and windy, and thus

A worker at the Libby Waipiʻo plantation in 1941 removes crowns from fruit before loading it into lug boxes.

Pineapple slips are trimmed before they are left to dry in the field for two weeks. Slips form on the peduncle, the stem that supports the pineapple fruit. Like suckers and fruit crowns, slips are used for planting.

The first manager's estate at the Libby plantation on Maunaloa, Molokaʻi, viewed here in 1931, is surrounded by pineapple fields. It served later as a guest house and then was torn down. In 2004, the lot where this home stood was vacant.

Kolo Wharf on the south coast of West Molokaʻi, seen here in a 1943 photo, was built by Libby to ship pineapple to the cannery on Oʻahu. It was replaced by the deeper harbor in Kaunakakai and later burned, rendering it unusable.

far had not been considered suitable for pineapple. Libby, after having seen the success of the crop on the dry areas of Central Oʻahu, decided the gentle slopes would serve as good pineapple land. The company's only previous direct contact with Molokaʻi was the shipment to its cannery of some fruit grown near Hālawa, on the wetter east end of the island, by independent growers.

Libby leased 2,850 acres near Maunaloa from the American Sugar Company on January 1, 1923. Elevations ranged from 500 to 1,300 feet. A dirt ranch road connected the area with Kaunakakai, 20 miles away. Libby landed equipment, supplies, and housing materials on the beach at Pāpōhaku and began preparing its first 1,000 acres for planting. It built a large residential camp in a central location and commenced work on its own wharf at Kolo, on the southwest coast of the island, considerably nearer than Kaunakakai.

Much of the land on the island's central plains was set aside for native Hawaiian homesteaders. In 1926 Libby began arranging with the homesteaders to grow pineapple on their properties. By 1932, one hundred twenty-seven homesteaders were involved. But the figure stabilized at seventy-eight in 1944, with 2,600 farmable acres. By 1965, Libby had a total of 12,500 acres in pineapple on Moloka'i, 9,000 acres on Maunaloa, and 3,500 in the Ho'olehua area.

Dole bought Libby's operations in 1970, and continued running the plantation for two years before deciding to close it. The phaseout was completed by 1975.

Libby on Maui.

Libby moved onto Maui in 1926 with the purchase of the Pauwela Pineapple Company, which had been founded in 1919 and built its concrete cannery structure in 1920. The purchase also involved leases on 3,774 acres and 961 acres of fee land. Additionally, there was a number of growers' contracts. At one point, Libby had as many as three hundred growers, but by 1931, there were about sixty-five growers farming 1,000 acres. Libby bought another 750 acres and leased 1,118 acres in 1930, all in the Makawao area. After World War II, the firm bought another 500 acres near the Maui cannery.

Production was two hundred thousand cases in 1926 and increased to 1.25 million cases during the 1950s. But as high production costs and cheap foreign competition began eating into Hawaiian pineapple markets, Libby decided to close its Maui operation in 1962. The Hasenroth Company, of Cleveland, operated the cannery for a short time, taking fruit from growers only. Hasenroth had been involved with the Hawaiian Canneries Company on Kaua'i, which also closed in 1962.

Libby had operated 21,000 acres on three plantations. It was the second largest pineapple company in Hawai'i and was the first of the large pineapple firms to leave the Islands. The nationwide food company was partly owned by the Swiss giant Nestlé, which took control in the 1970s. Libby had operated twenty-six food products' factories around the country in the 1950s, but by 1980, 100 years after its founding, it was closed.

BALDWIN PACKERS, LTD. (1923–1962)

Henry P. Baldwin had planned to grow sugar. He acquired land on West Maui and held it under the name Honolua Ranch, raising cattle and growing coffee pending the start of his sugar venture. After his death, the trustees of his estate decided to try pineapple instead. They hired David T. Fleming, who had five years of experience in pineapple with the Maui Agricultural Company's Grove Ranch. He was named manager in 1912 and planted his first 20 acres of pine in the summer of that year. A cannery and can-making plant were built at Honolua. The first pack in 1914 was 6,000 cases. It was transported to Lahaina on Pioneer Mill Company's sugar cane train tracks. In 1920, the plant was moved to Lahaina to be nearer Māla Wharf. Baldwin Packers Ltd. was incorporated in 1923 with capital of $1.5 million. Honolua Ranch transferred 15,550 acres of farmland, ranch, waste, and forest land to the new company. Alexander & Baldwin was named sales agent. New land was cleared at Honokōhau at the northern tip of West Maui, and proved to be excellent pineapple land.

The Baldwin Packers Lahaina cannery was closed in 1962. Baldwin Packers thereafter shipped its fruit by truck to the Kahului cannery of the Maui Pineapple Company, which had the same owners as Baldwin Packers.

KAUAI PINEAPPLE COMPANY (1906–1964)

McBryde Sugar Company, itself just seven years old, formed the Kauai Fruit and Land Company in 1906 for the production of pineapple. The name was more hopeful than accurate, since the company owned no land. It built a cannery in Lāwaʻi, and changed its name to the Kauai Pineapple Company. The firm was managed by Walter D. McBryde, the son of the founder of McBryde Sugar. On Walter McBryde's death, R. G. Bell became manager. He saw the firm through the Depression, when dividends were suspended, but the company survived and was able to resume dividend payments as well as to spend considerable sums to improve cannery and field equipment. In 1943 Bell was transferred to the Honolulu headquarters of Alexander & Baldwin, which by then operated Kauai Pine. J.G. Watkins was named to succeed Bell, and remained through his retirement in 1956. He was followed by Wayne Gregg, who remained through the company's closing.

In 1944 Grove Farm Company, which had land but no cannery, planted between 50 and 180 acres annually for Kauai Pineapple Company from 1945 to 1960, and became a minority stockholder in the firm. Several small growers also delivered fruit to the cannery.

Kauai Pine was continually under pressure for pineapple land from the larger sugar companies, new housing developments, and the hilly nature of what land remained. The company farmed some of the steepest lands available, and both extremely dry land on government leases in Hanapēpē and very wet properties leased from the Knudsen Estate in the area known as Knudsen Gap. Tractors sometimes were linked to each other by cables to keep them upright on the steepest slopes. Despite great persistence and innovation under Gregg's leadership, the firm could not survive. It was closed in 1964, and the cannery equipment was sold to the new plantations around the world that were challenging Hawai'i production.

HAWAIIAN CANNERIES COMPANY LTD. (1913–1962)

Albert Horner Sr., who was active in the early days of pineapple, headed a Honolulu group that opened Hawaiian Canneries on Kaua'i. The firm built a small two-line cannery in Kapa'a the first year and packed nineteen thousand cases with fruit from both growers and the company's own fields. Grove Farm Company began growing pineapples for the company in 1949, starting with 33 ⅓ acres that year, 95 acres in 1950, and 100 acres each year thereafter until Grove Farm gave up pineapple in 1960.

The Hasenroth Company, a Cleveland food company, was an early stockholder in Hawaiian Canneries. The company marketed the fruit and expanded its interest to become a major stockholder. In 1922, Henry Hasenroth approached Amfac's Lihue Plantation Company, which owned land near Hawaiian Canneries, and asked to acquire land in exchange for stock in Hawaiian Canneries. Amfac agreed on the condition that it be named agent for Hawaiian Canneries. As such, Amfac would be paid 1 percent on sales, 1 percent on purchases, and 6 percent on cash advances. With this arrangement in place, the 1930s Depression resulted in Amfac owning 90 percent of the company. By 1938, Hawaiian Canneries had an overdraft of $343,000 to Amfac, but the orders of the military in World War II turned the tide. By 1945, the company had a credit balance of $589,000 and paid dividends of $67,250. Ten years later, the company was in debt once more. It closed in 1962.

In 1979, after losing $7 million on its sugar operations the year before, Amfac tried planting some pineapple near Kapa'a for the fresh-fruit market, but the effort was abandoned after two years. Hasenroth tried running the Libby cannery on Maui for a short time, using pineapple bought from independent growers, but that attempt also failed.

HAWAIIAN FRUIT PACKERS LTD. (1936–1973)

The Depression affected the growers as well as the canning firms. When Hawaiian Canneries and Kauai Pine were unable to sell their canned fruit, and refused to buy the crops of Japanese growers near Kapa'a, the farmers organized their own firm, the Growers' Canning Association. The 1932 firm, with capital supplied by Randolph Crossley, built a cannery in the Kapa'a homestead area. But it was an extremely tough time for marketing pineapple, and by 1936, the company was in serious financial trouble. Crossley took over the firm to protect his investment and changed the name to Hawaiian Fruit Packers Ltd. Independent growers were producing about 25 percent of the company's fruit, with the remaining three-quarters coming from its own fields. In 1939, Crossley arranged with Stokely-Van Camp, a major nationwide food packer, for the exclusive distribution of the cannery's entire output. Crossley expanded the cannery that year with equipment bought from the defunct Kohala Pineapple Company.

The canning gear had been idle since 1931. In 1939 Crossley and manager Dorsey Edwards also approached Grove Farm to suggest it grow pineapple for the cannery. And, in 1941, Grove Farm started planting. It continued only through 1944, when Grove Farm began planting for Kauai Pine instead. With the closing of Kauai Pineapple, its manager, Wayne Gregg, moved to Hawaiian Fruit Packers, which he ran through its closing in 1973.

GROVE FARM COMPANY LTD. (1941–1960)

Grove Farm Company grew crops for all three major Kaua'i pineapple canning operations. The company had been in sugar for many years, but had land available for other uses and was actively experimenting with alternative crops. Grove Farm's pineapple plantings started at 50 acres with fruit delivered to Hawaiian Fruit Packers. It stopped planting for that canner in 1944, but the final crop was delivered in 1946.

In 1945 Grove Farm planted 44 acres for delivery to Kauai Pine, and moved up to 180 acres thereafter. In 1949, Grove Farm put in 33 1/3 acres of pineapple whose fruit would be sold to Hawaiian Canneries. The acreage grew to 50 acres in 1950 and 100 acres annually thereafter through 1960.

Hurricane Nina in 1957, the sugar strike in 1958, and Hurricane Dot in 1960 all hurt Grove Farm and the company reduced the size of its operations. Pineapple was a victim. In 1960 Grove Farm ended its relationship with the canneries and dropped pineapple.

PACIFIC PINEAPPLE COMPANY (1946–1957)

With the exception of Kohala Sugar's pineapple experiment, Pacific Pineapple Company was the only firm to get started in the business after World War II. The firm was incorporated in 1946 with plantings at Ho'olehua on Moloka'i. It had no cannery but delivered fruit to Dole's Honolulu cannery by barge. Randolph Crossley of Kaua'i's Hawaiian Fruit Packers was initially involved in the general supervision of the plantation, but ended his involvement in 1950. P. E. Spalding Jr. was company president and Eric Reppun the local manager at the company's Kala'e headquarters. The company sought production of 25,000 tons per year on land it leased directly and used through arrangements with Hawaiian homesteaders. Pacific Pineapple closed in 1957.

Olympic swimmer and Hawaiian icon Duke Kahanamoku (left) and television star Arthur Godfrey (in hat facing Kahanamoku) participate in a pineapple industry publicity tour. Libby executive Verne Hass (center) holds pineapple upside-down and Maunaloa plantation manager Harry Larson (right) holds a cut pineapple.

The Associations

W uring its century in the sun Hawaiian pineapple was represented by two kinds of associations, although there was some overlap between the two: organizations that primarily marketed the crop and ones that conducted research. The first, the Pineapple Growers' Association was formed by James Dole after the depression of 1907 cut sales and left growers with large inventories. This association, formed in 1908 and active through 1912, was meant to promote Hawaiian pineapple on the Mainland. Only the Hawaiian Islands Packing Company and Captain Cook Fruit Company failed to join.

The Hawaiian Islands Packers Association was formed in 1912 to market pineapple, promote cooperation in various areas, and to support research. Its name was changed in 1922 to the Association of Hawaiian Pineapple Canners, and it remained in business until 1933. But the Great Depression pointed out the need for a more active marketing organization, and in 1932, the industry formed the Pineapple Producers Cooperative Association, Ltd. The next year, the AHPC, along with its research staff and experiment station, was merged into the PPCA.

A decade later, the industry felt it needed something different, and formed the Pineapple Growers Association of

Hawai'i "to perform appropriate trade association activities in interest of the industry, such as statistical services, advertising, market research and representation of the industry with government agencies."

Dr. F. G. Krauss, a Maui homesteader who grew pineapple, conducted some of the important early research on the crop on his own homestead at Ha'ikū. He was the father of Beatrice Krauss, whose own contributions to pineapple research would later be quite important. The elder Krauss conducted research on his land from 1913 to 1922. The Krauss homestead was later converted into a substation of the Hawaiian Agricultural Experiment Station.

The Hawaiian Sugar Planters Association and fertilizer companies began conducting pineapple research in early 1914. Later, the Hawaiian Pineapple Packers Association also gave its support to research projects. The Pineapple Department of the HSPA existed from 1914 to 1923, and Dr. H. L. Lyon was assigned to conduct the research work. In 1917, the HPPA rented two acres at Wahiawā and in 1919 added 89 acres at Kapālama-Uka, both for pineapple research.

In 1923, the sugar planters association established a pineapple experiment station at Wahiawā, financed through the AHPC. R. E. Doty, an associate of Lyon, was placed in charge. Growers faced problems with wilt, various diseases, nematodes, and other production issues. The need for research was critical. The Wahiawā site was quickly outgrown, and the AHPC established a larger research facility with headquarters on the Mānoa campus of the University of Hawai'i. Doty returned to working in sugar research, and L. A. Dean, the university president, was named part-time director of the pineapple research program in 1924. He took over full time in 1926, holding the position through his resignation in 1930. Dr. Royal

N. Chapman directed the station after Dean's departure. And in 1939, J. L. Collins was named acting director, a position he held through several changes in the organization until 1945.

In 1933, the Pineapple Producers Cooperative Association assumed control of the research station, which, through 1941, was called the Experiment Station of the PPCA. From 1941 to 1945, it was called the Pineapple Research Institute and operated as a department of the PPCA. The PPCA was dissolved during the war years and replaced by the Pineapple Growers' Association of Hawai'i. The Pineapple Research Institute of Hawai'i became a separate organization and began consolidating pineapple research work that had been performed by the separate pineapple companies.

Each pineapple grower contributed to the PRI in an amount proportional to its pineapple production—the same kind of arrangement under which the sugar industry funded the HSPA. E. C. Auchter was named director of the new institute in 1945, and held the job through 1952, when he resigned. Robert L. Cushing took the post through 1963. Sterling Wortman had the post in 1964 and 1965. W. G. Sanford directed PRI in 1966 and 1967, and J. B. Smith ran it from 1967 to 1971.

PRI was reduced in size and scope in 1966 as the pineapple industry in Hawai'i began facing serious financial constraints. Only a skeleton staff remained, and in 1968, PRI left its longtime home at the University of Hawai'i at Mānoa and moved to the Wahiawā field station. By 1971, PRI's membership included only Dole, Del Monte, and the Maui Pineapple Company, then Dole announced it planned to discontinue participation. The remaining two companies kept on for another year, but in 1972, PRI was dissolved. Several pineapple scientists became part of the University of Hawai'i staff, which conducted some of its own pineapple research.

A pineapple executive holding a characteristic curved pineapple knife makes inspections in an O'ahu field. Pearl Harbor lies in the background.

PINEAPPLE RESEARCH ACHIEVEMENTS

While Hawai'i is among the best pineapple growing areas in the world, the problems with commercial production were such that the industry would not have survived without an aggressive agricultural research effort, both in the field and in the cannery.

The canneries could not have handled the increased tonnage being produced in the fields had it not been for the 1913 development of the Ginaca Automatic Pineapple Machine. The Ginaca, as it was commonly called, initially processed 35 fruits per minute, replacing much slower hand coring and peeling.

In 1920, the industry developed the eradicator, which scraped excess flesh from the discarded peels. The flesh was used to produce juice.

Ha'ikū Fruit and Packing Company produced clarified juice in 1907, a product later improved upon by Hapco and other firms.

Frozen pineapple concentrate was developed in 1952.

Hapco's Dr. E. G. Felton invented a way to recover pineapple sugar using an ion-exchange method.

The cannery residue was dried and converted into pineapple bran for cattle feed.

Factories recovered citric acid for sale and extracted the enzyme bromelain, a meat tenderizer, from the stems of pineapple plants. Bromelain is also used in beer brewing and helps reduce the formation of scar tissue.

The industry learned to remove flavor esters from pineapple juice and then reintroduce them during the concentrate process to improve flavor.

In the fields around 1900, many of the plants were chlorotic, meaning their leaves were pale and the plants appeared unhealthy. In 1915, Territorial Experiment Station researcher M. Johnson found that the condition was due to an iron deficiency in the plants. The high levels of manganese in the soil was making the iron unavailable to the plants. Growers resolved the problem by spraying iron directly on the leaves.

In 1926, researchers determined that a disease called yellow spot was caused by a virus transmitted by the insect Thrips tabaci. The insect's host plant, a plant that helped it go through its normal life cycle, was the common weed called *Emilia* or red pualele. In 1949, researchers recommended growers control the weed in order to stamp out the disease.

As early as 1915, growers of other crops used strips of tar paper in their fields to reduce soil moisture, control weeds, and keep the soil warm. Pineapple growers began using the technique regularly in 1922, rolling out long strips of paper and planting new pineapple slips right through them.

Pineapple wilt was a serious problem that showed up with the first crops produced in Hawai'i in the 1800s. Growers recognized that ants were somehow involved, and by the 1920s they were using heroic measures to try to control ants and limit their access to the fields. Some built ditches entirely around their fields and filled them with oil. Others built fences coated with oil and sticky compounds.

The wilt was a serious enough problem that some growers were already looking for foreign areas free of the wilt, where they could grow pineapples. Jerome Beatty, writing in the American magazine in 1939, said, "by 1930...all seemed lost, and three important growers prepared to leave the Islands, one planted experimental fields in Fiji, one investigated Africa, one

Crews lay mulch paper by hand in the early 1920s. The edges of the paper would be covered with soil and new plants were inserted along both edges of the paper to form double rows.

A bedding machine lays mulch paper and applies fertilizer on three rows at a time, modernizing the old manual technique shown above. The black mulch paper was replaced in later years by black plastic.

Field workers stand by a mule-drawn spray rig in the 1920s.

Pineapple worker sprays insecticide by hand.

was ready to try the Philippines. They had thousands of dollars into research with no results."

Pineapple Research Institute scientist Walter Carter, who had joined the organization in 1930, determined that mealybugs were directly infecting plants with the wilt virus, although ants were clearly involved. Carter wrote:

> This ant is the mealybug's nursemaid, garbage can and police force all at the same time; it moves the mealybug around, to permit it to establish itself on succulent leaves, removes the surplus wax and other excretions from the mealybug's body and vigorously defends it against enemies. The mealybug, on the other hand, while accepting these attentions, provides a good deal of food for the ant in the way of surplus wax and the tiny globules of honey dew which are secreted from glands in the mealybug's body.

He also noted that several species of ants sometimes worked the same mealybugs.

Carter began studying sprays that could be used to control the bugs. Early formulation of oil emulsion sprays worked but were very expensive. Later he developed a spray of diesel oil and absorbent clay—it was cheaper, and it killed the bugs. In the 1940s, insecticides began appearing on the scene, and the one that worked best was DDT (*dicholoro-diphenyl-tricholoroethane*). It was effective on contact, and it was widely used for insect control around the world. However, DDT was later banned because of its residual negative impact on many creatures it was not intended to affect. Other, less hazardous compounds became available in later years.

Nematodes, tiny worms that form nodules in the roots of plants which weakens them, were another early problem for the pineapple industry. Maxwell Johnson found that the chem-

A labor crew walks through a year-old pineapple field during the 1940s, spraying for mealybugs.

ical chloropicrin helped control them. In 1940, Walter Carter and Carl T. Schmidt discovered the chemical DD (*dicholoro-propene dicholoro-propane*) provided nematode control.

PRI researcher Kanjyo Sakimura developed a control for another soil pest, the white grub of the anomala beetle.

One of the major challenges for the pineapple industry was its seasonal fruiting. All the plants produced fruit at once, requiring large factory capacity that was unused for much of the year and a large seasonal labor force. If plants could be forced to fruit over a more extended time, both factory and labor could be used more effectively. In 1903 growers in the Azores Islands had made an astonishing discovery. Woodsmoke used to heat hothouses made pineapple plants

Promoting Pineapples

All graphics in this section are taken from the DeSoto Brown Collection.

Postcards show Dole Cannery tour guides with the landmark rooftop pineapple water tower (from the 1950s, left) and two bikini-clad young women lounging in the fields (from the 1960s, above).

A comic postcard from the 1950s showcases a fruit so gargantuan that it must be transported on a truck; similarly silly cards were published as early as 1915.

"Libby's Hawaiian Pineapple Girl" smiles bravely as she cuddles up to a prickly pineapple in about 1915 (left). Nature's blessings are amply displayed in this often-reprinted Dole photo postcard shot by William Pitchford around 1955 (right).

The Association of Hawaiian Pineapple Canners printed these booklets (left and center) in the 1920s. A prepublication contest soliciting recipes for the middle one received an amazing 60,000 submissions. The Dole booklet on the right, from about 1931, explains the company's three grades of canned pineapple.

The "we" in the title of this 1914 Hawaiian Pineapple Packers' Association booklet are fifteen well-known female cooks of the time, many of whom wrote regular columns for women's magazines.

The montage of various Hawaiian Pineapple Company labels (opposite) was published in a 1923 brochure, "By Nature Crowned". Elaborate, colorful labels dating from about 1910 into the 1950s show a variety of motifs. Movie star Dorothy Lamour's appearance on the Lalani example promotes a 1952 Hollywood film, "The Greatest Show On Earth" (above).

National magazine ads for Dole from the 1930s and 1940s use Hawaiian imagery (hula dancers, surfing) as well as a good dose of glamour seen in the well-dressed party guests at top right, and lovely Hollywood performer Raquel Torres in center-right.

Advertisements from 1957, 1926, 1925, and the middle 1930s emphasize that the best quality pineapple always originates in Hawai'i (clockwise from top). Everyone's Hawaiian dream: Diamond Head, happy hula dancers, and pineapple chunks, from 1954 (following page).

DOLE
HAWAIIAN
PINEAPPLE CHUNKS
IN EXTRA HEAVY SYRUP
CONTENTS 1 LB. 4 OZ.

produce fruit buds. PRI researcher Gordon Nightingale perfected the use of several forcing agents to initiate fruiting.

In the early 1930s, Dr. C. P. Sideris and Beatrice Krauss developed the practice of applying nutrients directly to the leaves of the plants, a process now universally practiced and termed foliar fertilization.

The labor shortage caused by World War II limited the availability of workers for pineapple weed control, and in 1944, PRI researcher R. K. Tam developed the first effective chemical weed control, combining diesel oil, spreading agents, and sodium pentachlorophenate.

From the 1940s until irrigation became the norm, growers on many plantations began using the trash from previous crops as mulch between the pineapple beds. It controlled weeds and helped retain soil moisture, which was very important on the drier plantations. Ultimately, drip irrigation allowed growers to include fertilizers and pest control chemicals in their water, improving their effectiveness.

After 1960, researchers developed the use of Ethrel to more effectively force plants to produce fruit buds and virtually ripened fruits on command. Fruitone reduced the size of the crowns and enlarged the fruits. The chemical Maintain helped speed the propagation of planting material. A range of fungicides, nematicides, and insecticides were developed, many of them to replace chemicals like DDT, which were discovered to be harmful to the environment.

Here, suckers are used as planting material. Suckers grow from the stump of the pineapple plant. Slips, which grow from the stem below the fruit, and the crowns atop the fruit, are also employed for planting.

Pineapple Plantation Practices

I n the early days, in order to farm pineapple, growers often had to clear fields that often had not been previously used for agriculture. Hand labor removed brush and trees, and large stones were hauled out using teams of mules hitched to flat pieces of sheet metal that served as sleds. Later, tractors were used to push boulders into ravines or into centralized piles of stones. Many such piles can still be seen in old plantation fields.

Early plowing was often performed with a single disk plow attached to a three-mule team with a man driving the mules. Such a team could plow about a half an acre in a day. The plows would be followed by mule-drawn disk harrows that would break up the large chunks of soil and prepare it for planting.

A mule team with a small plow would lay out lines for planting. In the early days, plants were laid out in single rows. Later, double rows, and occasionally triple rows, were planted. Fertilizer and mulch paper were applied by hand. Initially, mulching paper and fertilizer were seldom used, but they later became a common practice.

Each planting row or bed, was about 4 3/4 feet wide. Planting blocks consisted of 23-27 beds depending on the size of farm equipment. To the side of planting blocks were roads used by harvesting and spraying equipment whose booms reached halfway into the blocks. Lengths of planting blocks varied by the size of the field and the location of crossroads.

Today, fields are subsoiled (breaking up the soil below normal plowing depth), plowed, and disked. A bedding machine applies preplanting fertilizer, nematode fumigants, and lays down the plastic sheeting that has replaced mulch paper. Drip irrigation lines are sometimes installed under the plastic in the centers of the beds. Fumigation of the soil is sometimes replaced by application of chemicals through drip irrigation lines.

While much experimentation has gone into developing a pineapple planting machine, no equipment has been as effective as hand planting. However, the method of handling planting material has been improved, so that it now takes less than half the manpower to plant a field than was required in the past.

Weeds were once controlled through the use of mule-drawn cultivators working between the rows of pineapple plants, but such techniques became overly expensive. Now, while some spot-spraying of herbicides by individual workers is sometimes employed, herbicides are commonly applied with large boom sprayers, which span half the width of a planting block in a field and are driven down both sides of the block to cover the entire planting area. Other chemicals, including insecticides, fertilizers, and forcing agents are often applied with the same machines, although nozzle arrangements may be changed to direct the spray onto the plants rather than the areas between them.

A pineapple farmer in the 1920s breaks soil with two mules and a plow.

A *multipurpose trash-mulch machine* in 1955 tills the soil, lays mulch paper, fumigates for nematodes, and fertilizes, while retaining mulch from the previous crop between rows for weed control and moisture retention.

Pineapple field spray rigs during the 1930s were most often drawn by mules, although this one appears to be pulled by a horse.

A long boom supported by cables allows a motorized spray rig to cover a wide section of pineapple field.

RIGHT: Spray trucks work adjacent roads, their booms sweeping the fields with pesticides.

In this 1959 photo, a spray truck applies insecticide on an Oʻahu field.

Spray biplane cruises low over pineapple fields, applying iron sulfate to correct a nutritional deficiency in the plants.

Harvesting machines with crews walking between pineapple rows behind long conveyor belts in Waipi'o, O'ahu, in 1956. Workers break pineapple fruits off plants, remove crowns, and place the fruits on the conveyor belt, which carries them to a truck.

Field worker in 1930s or early 1940s removes crowns from the harvested
fruit before putting them in lug boxes for transport to the factory.

Harvested fruit lies at the side of the dirt plantation road in 1941, waiting for crews to remove crowns and load them into lug boxes.

Early fertilizing units were mule-drawn 30-gallon tanks with spray arms that covered about 18 feet and required two human operators. Modern tractor-drawn sprayers may have one or two booms that cover half a block (often more than 50 feet) each. They hold 500 to 1,000 gallons of chemical, and can be refilled from tanker trucks without having to stop.

Harvesting was done by hand through the early 1950s. It was an arduous process. Pickers would first walk through the fields, breaking pineapple fruits off the plants, and removing the crowns. They would leave the fruit atop the bed and move on. Later, they would return with a canvas shoulder bag and collect the fruits, which were carried to the end of the 200-foot long pineapple beds and placed on the ground. Other workers picked up the fruit and placed it in lug boxes, each of which held about 60 pounds of pineapple. Workers picked up the lug boxes by hand and put them on the wagons drawn by mules. The wagons held forty boxes. The wagons would be offloaded by hand onto rail cars, trucks, or taken directly to the wharf or factory. For neighbor island plantations without canneries, lug boxes were placed on sixty-box skips and loaded by hoist onto barges for shipment to Honolulu canneries.

Today, much of the operation is mechanized, but the fruit is still hand-picked. Harvesting crews walk side-by-side through the fields, following a truck-mounted conveyor boom that spans half the field. Fruits are picked, crowns removed, and fruits placed on the conveyor belt, which carries them into a large bulk-box mounted on the back of a truck that is linked to the harvester. The boxes have a capacity of 4.5 tons of fruit. When the box is full, the truck drives off and is replaced by another. The bulk-box is loaded by finger lift onto a transport truck capable of carrying four boxes. At the harbor, cranes pick up and move the bulk-boxes. The newer system, in which individual fruits are not handled between picking and the factory, reduces bruising.

Before the Ginaca machine, pineapples were shelled on a manually operated machine called a Jastrow. A fruit was placed on a spike and shoved through a revolving knife. The ends were cut off by hand, and then transferred to another machine that removed the core. The Jastrow was improved and made semi-automatic, but fruits still needed to be handled through the various stages. As a result, the system could process no more than ten fruits per minute. Employees would feed the skins individually through spiked rollers that removed the remaining flesh.

A pallet full of lug boxes is hoisted by crane to a barge for transport to the Honolulu cannery.

A *pineapple grower with a modest farm hauls fruit by pack animal.*

Growers on Maui deliver fruit in horse-drawn wagons during the 1920s.

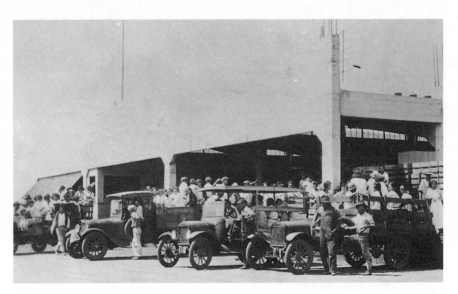

While smaller growers still used horses and mules to haul crops to the factory, some were already using trucks, as seen here on Maui during the 1920s.

Lug boxes full of fruit arrive at the canning plant in the years before large truck-mounted bins were used.

Fruit arrives at the factory preparation department in the 1950s, hauled in bins aboard trucks.

The multi-function Ginaca machine as it looked from 1910 to 1915.

The Ginaca in operation during the period from 1915 to 1948.

Sizing machine removes shell from the cylinder of yellow fruit.

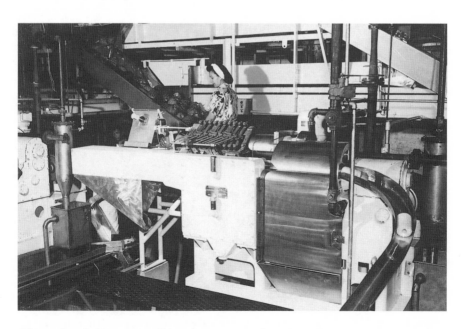

The updated Ginaca machine design, seen here in 1953.

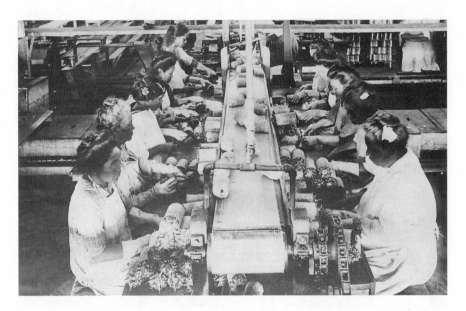

The pineapple factory trimming table, in an era when women sat at the table and wore flowers in their hair.

Pineapple trimming line in the 1960s. Cannery workers in uniform use sharp pineapple knives to remove imperfections on fruit cylinders.

Rotary pineapple slicing blades are offset to reduce pressure on the fruit cylinder.

The packing table, where female cannery workers filled cans with slices of pineapple.

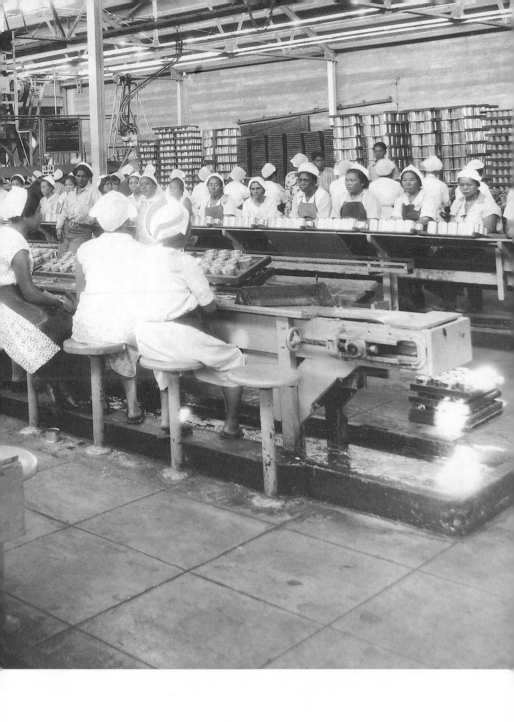

Belt-driven equipment powered from pulleys and shafts overhead predated a pineapple-processing department where individual units were powered by their own electric motors.

Hundreds of cans running down conveyor belts are stacked in a cannery processing department during the 1960s.

Aerial view of the Libby cannery in Kalihi on O'ahu, with Kamehameha Highway on right and Waiakamilo Road at top.

A crew oversees the cooking of the canned fruit.

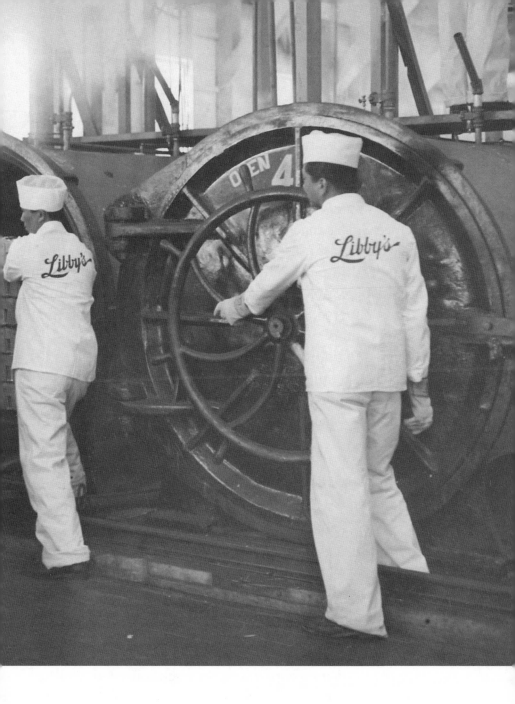

The first Ginaca machine was developed about 1915. It sized the fruit and cut the shell off. Then, the pineapple cylinder was manually moved to the main part of the machine which removed the ends and core. The machine also had a device called an eradicator that removed flesh from skins automatically.

Once Ginaca machines were put in use, trucks delivered pineapples in loads of five boxes to the machines. Later, fruit was manually dumped from lug boxes onto a conveyor system that carried pineapples to the Ginaca machines. Now, bulk-boxes are delivered to a hydraulic unloading station that dumps fruits onto a conveyor. Fruits are graded into three sizes and delivered to appropriate Ginaca machines.

In 1949, a fully automatic Ginaca was developed. It removes skins and delivers pineapples by air pressure to a device that removes the ends and cores and cuts the flesh from the skins.

Workers still trim the resulting fruits by hand using knives to remove skin residue and defects in the fruit. Trimmers initially worked on wooden tables, but now they are made of stainless steel.

Pineapples used to be cut into slices with a gang knife, which consisted of several attached blades that were pressed by hand through the fruit. Today's slicers are fully automatic. Trimmed pineapples are delivered to a machine that has rotating knives on an arbor. It cuts the pineapples into slices and delivers them to the packing table.

In the industry's early days, the pack consisted of either slices or crushed pineapple. Today there are slices, chunks, tidbits, crushed pineapple, and pineapple juice. Early canners packed pineapple in water, but later used sugared juice syrup.

Today pineapples are mainly packed in plain juice. Juice itself was first packed in the early 1930s and developed into one of the main products of the industry. Today, rather than straight juice, the industry mostly produces frozen juice concentrate.

Packers canned their product in the late 1800s and early 1900s in cans whose tops were then soldered closed. Sanitary cans introduced in the early 1910s no longer required hand soldering. The filled cans were then cooked in hot water vats and removed to cooling water vats. The machine that closed the cans initially processed about thirty cans a minute.

Today, equipment can close 150 to 350 cans per minute. Cans are then processed in an agitating spiral cooker and cooler. Some factories use a roller-spinner cooler.

Hand labeling and wooden cases marked the early industry. Those cases were later replaced by lighter, wire-tied veneer cases. Today, the cans are packed in cardboard boxes. Hand labeling was replaced by movable machines that were delivered to the stacks of bright cans. Today, the cans are either directly labeled after processing, or delivered to a central labeling station.

Hand trucks and hand stacking of cases in the warehouse have been replaced by boxes stacked on pallets and moved with forklift units.

UNSWEETENED
PINEAPPLE JUICE
from Hawaii

This is the unsweetened juice of sun-ripened Hawaiian Pineapple—pineapple picked at peak-flavor goodness. It is a good source of Vitamins C and B_1.

Serving Suggestions

Serve well-chilled as a beverage or use in punches, sherbets, gelatin salads, and desserts.

MADE IN U. S. A.

Pineapple can labels.

HAWAIIAN REFRESHER

Libby's Pineapple Spears add a glamour touch to fruit punches, pineapple juice or any favorite beverage containing fruit juice. Try them as a good-eating garnish for Pineapple Gingerale Punch. Combine equal parts chilled Libby's Pineapple Juice and chilled gingerale. Pour over ice or sherbet. Garnish with pineapple spears.

PINEAPPLE-APPLE SALAD

Alternate chilled Libby's Pineapple Spears with slices of bright red apple on salad greens. (Dip apple slices in pineapple syrup to prevent darkening.) For variety, use avocado slices, Libby's Grapefruit and Orange Sections or Libby's Sliced Cling Peaches in place of apple slices. Garnish with pimiento cheese spread, if desired.

Libby's from **Hawaii**

NET WEIGHT 1 LB. 4½ OZ.
581 GRAMS

PACKED IN HAWAII
BY
Libby, McNeill & Libby
HONOLULU, HAWAII

• Can Size . . . . NO. 2
• Amount . . . . . 16 SPEARS
• Servings . . . . 4 TO 5

These spears are cut from sun-ripened Hawaiian Pineapple. Picked when fully ripe, the pineapple is quick-canned to preserve its peak-flavor goodness.

Serving Suggestions

Serve as a breakfast fruit or a dessert. Use in salads, desserts, or hot with meat.

MADE IN U.S.A.

Libby's **PINEAPPLE SPEARS** IN EXTRA HEAVY SYRUP

PINEAPPLE SPEARS IN EXTRA HEAVY SYRUP

Libby's **PINEAPPLE PIE FILLING**

HAWAIIAN PINEAPPLE PIE

Line an 8-inch pie pan with pastry, allowing ½ inch to hang over edge. Pour in Libby's Pineapple Pie Filling. Cover with top crust or strips of pastry. Seal edge by folding up allowance. Flute rim or press with tines of fork. Bake in a hot oven (425° F.) 30 to 35 minutes. 6 servings.

PINEAPPLE TOPPING

Simmer Libby's Pineapple Filling in heavy saucepan 2 minutes. Serve as a sauce with ham or as a dessert topping.

Libby's **PINEAPPLE PIE FILLING** from **Hawaii** READY TO USE

NET WEIGHT 1 LB. 5½ OZ.
610 GRAMS

PINEAPPLE PIE FILLING

INGREDIENTS
DICED PINEAPPLE, SUGAR, WATER, STARCH, LEMON JUICE, SALT AND ARTIFICIAL FLAVORING

PACKED IN HAWAII
BY
Libby, McNeill & Libby
HONOLULU, HAWAII

• Can size . . . . . . No. 2
• Amount approx. 2¼ cups
• Makes . . . 1 8-inch pie

This ready-to-use pie filling is packed from Libby's sunripened Hawaiian Pineapple. It has been carefully thickened and sweetened to make an excellent pineapple pie.

SERVING SUGGESTIONS
Use for pies, tarts, cobblers and filled cookies. Also delicious served over ice cream, waffles, cake, pudding or as a garnish with ham entrees.

MADE IN U.S.A.

LEMON-PINEAPPLE SHERBET

Combine 1½ cups sugar, 1½ cups milk, ½ cup lemon juice (about 3 lemons) and 2 tbsp. grated lemon peel (about 1 lemon). Stir in 1 No. 2 can Libby's Crushed Pineapple, well drained. Fold in 1 cup whipping cream, whipped. Pour into refrigerator freezing trays and freeze with refrigerator set at coldest setting (about 4 hours). Stir once or twice during freezing. Makes approximately 3 pints. Garnish with toasted coconut.

CRUSHED PINEAPPLE-CARROT MOLD

Drain 1 No. 2 can Libby's Crushed Pineapple. Add enough water to pineapple syrup to make 1½ cups. Heat to a boil. Add 1 pkg. lemon-flavored gelatin; stir until dissolved. Add ½ cup sugar, ¼ tsp. salt, and 2 tbsp. lemon juice. Chill until slightly thickened. Add pineapple and 1 cup finely grated carrots. Whip ½ pint whipping cream stiff; fold into gelatin. Pour into 8" ring mold (1½ qts.); chill until firm. (For easy unmolding, make salad a day ahead of serv-

Libby's from **Hawaii**

NET WEIGHT 1 LB. 4½ OZ.
581 GRAMS

PACKED IN HAWAII
BY
Libby, McNeill & Libby
HONOLULU, HAWAII

• Can Size . . . . NO. 2
• Amount . . APPROX. 2¼ CUPS
• Servings . . APPROX. 4 TO 5

This pineapple is cut from sun-ripened Hawaiian Pineapple. Picked when fully ripe, the pineapple is quick-canned to preserve its peak-flavor goodness.

Serving Suggestions

Serve as a breakfast fruit or dessert. Use as a dessert topping and in salads.

MADE IN U.S.A.

Libby's **CRUSHED PINEAPPLE** IN EXTRA HEAVY SYRUP

CRUSHED PINEAPPLE IN EXTRA HEAVY SYRUP

Harvesting pineapple by hand in 1946. Note protective gear, a long-sleeved shirt, heavy trousers, and gloves for the pineapple thorns, and helmet for the subtropical sun.

Working Pine

Plantations built entire communities, self-contained villages that met virtually all of the residents' needs. There were cottages for married workers and quarters for bachelors. Housing might be a building with several rooms for bachelors, one for each worker, along side an individual unit for a family with the wife cooking and cleaning for the bachelors. Plantation housing for families was typically a rectangular structure with four or five rooms, often of single-walled wood frame construction. Supervisors normally got fancier houses on bigger lots. Employees normally paid rent for their homes, but the rent was extremely low by standards on the open market. Plantation towns often included hospitals or clinics staffed with nurses and doctors paid by the plantations, churches, ballparks, tennis courts, theaters, a pool hall, and more were built by the pineapple companies. Stores were run by the plantation or were sometimes leased to private operators. In later years, plantation schools were operated by the counties and the state.

The pineapple industry's work force mimicked the ethnic diversity of the rest of Hawai'i. Indeed, along with the sugar industry, it was responsible for some of that diversity since it brought in foreign workers to staff the plantations. Most of the

Labor camp at Waipiʻo, Oʻahu. The roads are dirt but the homes are well maintained.

imported labor of the last six decades came from the Philippines. The new immigrants tended to work in the field jobs. Japanese was the other major ethnic group working on the plantations. On their second generation in Hawai'i, they tended to work as supervisors, artisan-welders, mechanics, or in other specialty positions.

A Moloka'i plantation village in the 1950s had this ethnic breakdown.

Ethnicity/Detail	Male	Female	Children	Total
Filipino	306	54	124	484
Japanese	93	35	60	188
Caucasian	8	11	11	30
Puerto Rican	1	3	6	10
Portuguese	2	3	3	8
Chinese	4	1	0	5
Hawaiian	0	2	0	2
Mixed	7	24	103	134
Total	421	133	307	861

Plantation work was early work. Workers would awake at 3 to 4 A.M. to prepare their breakfast and put together a lunch, which was normally eaten in the field. The meals, frequently carried in dedicated containers called "kaukau tins," contained simple fare, including rice as a starch and some meat, either chicken or prepared meats such as Spam or Vienna Sausage.

In many communities, a whistle or horn loud enough to be heard throughout the village would blast to mark the time to start work. The turnout whistles went off at 5 or 6 A.M. and alerted employees that they had a half-hour to get to work. The work gangs of men and women would gather at dedicated turnout areas. Field workers would climb aboard personnel trucks to be driven to the field work areas. They broke at late morning for a half-hour lunch. Workers would sit in small groups, often sharing items from their individual lunch pails. Near the end of the day, Filipino workers would sometimes keep an eye out for the fruit of a plantation weed called bittermelon, which was often collected in the field to be eaten with the next day's meal. On occasion workers would cut the top off a pineapple fruit, mash the flesh inside with their plantation knives, and replace the top. A few days later, still in the field, the mash would have fermented and created an alcoholic refreshment for which they would return or which would be enjoyed by subsequent crews.

The work day was done early in the afternoon, and employees returned home at 2:30 or 3:30 P.M. Then, there was laundry to be done and gardens to be tended. Some men trained fighting cocks, which were pitted against other cocks on weekends. Workers lounged around the post office or the community store, played cards, and starting in the 1950s, watched television. By 8 P.M., the pineapple towns were deserted, with nearly everyone in bed.

Immigrant Filipino workers came from twenty different districts in the Philippines, but mostly from Ilocos Norte and Ilocos Sur, and spoke the Ilocano language. A smaller percentage, mainly from the Pangasinan and Visayan Islands, spoke Visayan, and still fewer were Tagalogs, the name of both the people and their language. However, Tagalog was the common language in which virtually all Filipino workers could converse.

There was also a distinct age classification among Filipino workers. The oldest group arrived on the Hawaiian plantations before 1931, and another large group arrived in

A *pineapple plantation town going-away party in* 1960. *The author is pictured against the dark background of the right door at center rear.*

1946. The older workers were almost all male and many were single. The 1946 group was younger and 75 percent of them were married.

Payday was an active day in the community, with cockfighting and other gambling, collections for community charities, and the activities of "Ripa" (raffle) women, who would sell raffle tickets for clothing and other wares, and would later dance and socialize, primarily with the single men.

Cockfighting went on regularly from the end of September to August, when the chickens molt. Although illegal, the gaming was conducted fairly openly in the plantation camps. Gambling was rampant whether on the chicken fights or at gaming tables where the Chinese games of Paikyao and Haikyu, Filipino Payut, and Western gin rummy and poker were played.

Filipino bands, groups of three or four playing on drums, saxophone, guitar, and mandolin, played dance music at festivities like Rizal Day, weddings, and baptisms. Favorite tunes were slow and sentimental.

Some Filipino workers were members of the Filipino Federation of America. The group's leader, Dr. Hilario Moncado, was an avid golfer, and many of his followers also played golf. Many workers were vegetarians, and others joked that while they couldn't drink regular milk, they could use Carnation milk, since it came from a flower.

At the Libby plantation on Moloka'i, some Filipino workers ate dog, preferably black dog, but this was enjoyed

This typical plantation house was the home of the Alfred Oshiro family at Maunaloa, Moloka'i.

infrequently—generally at single men's beach parties, accompanied by California sherry and Tokay wine.

Japanese workers had generally immigrated earlier than the Filipinos but even those born in Hawai'i preserved several Japanese customs. One was the *mochi*-pounding of New Year's Eve, which converted hot cooked *mochi* rice into a dough used to make confections for lavish New Year's Day feasts. Rice wine, *sake*, was in plentiful supply at such parties.

Older plantation camps had community bath houses used by Japanese workers. The children of Japanese-American workers generally attended Japanese language school twice a week in addition to regular school. Classes frequently were taught by the Buddhist minister, and the Japanese clubhouse would be used for a schoolroom.

The plantations provided virtually all the community facilities traditionally established by municipal governments in normal towns: a dispensary and company nurse or doctor, a post office building, clubhouses, tennis court, baseball park, poolroom, barbershop, movie theater, store, service station, and even the local school. Some of these facilities would be operated by private enterprises, but on company property and only with the approval of the company.

On some plantations, the living quarters for different ethnic groups were separated in the early years. But while there were specific ethnic gatherings, plantation employees often socialized without regard to race. Often, relations were based less on ethnic derivation than on plantation rank. For example, Hawai'i-born supervisors of Japanese ancestry regularly socialized with fellow supervisors of Caucasian descent.

Workers apply fertilizer directly to leaf bases of year-old pineapple plants.

Labor Organization

L abor organization in Hawai'i started in the early years of the century, and by 1935, there was increasing contact between Hawai'i labor leaders and those of the International Longshoremen's and Warehousemen's Union, the ILWU, on the West Coast. Labor unrest initially involved mostly Filipinos working on both sugar and pineapple plantations. Workers at the HC&S sugar plantation on Maui struck on April 19, 1937, keeping single workers off the job completely while allowing married men with children to continue to work but not participate in harvesting the cane. Ultimately, thirty-five hundred workers at three Maui plantations remained on strike for eighty-six days, until July 17, 1937.

The first pineapple-only strike was in mid-August 1937 on Moloka'i, although it was not a union operation, and the genesis of the walkout was somewhat vague. Three hundred California Packing Corporation (CPC) single workers went out first. They were required to leave plantation housing, and camped at a county park east of the old Kukui Theater in Kaunakakai. Libby workers left next and camped in the beach-front Kalama'ula coconut grove, where the CPC workers joined them. Eventually, more than a thousand single workers struck, all of them Filipino. They organized their strike camp, with a police force recognizable by white towels worn around the officers' necks. Neither the plantations nor Moloka'i police did anything to assist the workers. Their primary outside help came from the island's major landowner, Moloka'i Ranch Company. The strike lasted several weeks, and during that period, many of the strikers found other jobs. The strikes resulted in improved conditions for labor at these and other plantations, but companies generally continued to resist union activity.

The first recognized union in the agricultural field in Hawai'i was the United Canning, Agricultural, Packing and Allied Workers Association, the UCAPAWA, which organized non-agricultural workers at Kaua'i Pineapple Company. Manager R. A. "Dick" Bell did not oppose the organization, and the National Labor Relations Board-overseen vote was 162–10 in favor of the union. Jack Wayne Hall, a former seaman and waterfront organizer who had been with the sugar workers before the big Maui strike, worked for the UCAPAWA. However, the union was dismantled by the military during World War II and Kaua'i Pine once again became a non-organized plantation.

In 1944, the ILWU was back in Hawai'i, with Jack Hall as its regional director, helping sugar workers and ultimately those in other industries gain recognition. The union organized employees of fifty-seven companies in twelve different trades, including mill workers, pineapple field workers, pineapple cannery workers, engineers, cooks, laundry workers, guards, and truck drivers.

The main issues for the organizers: the feudal attitude of the plantations; racial segregation; the perquisite system that provided housing, medical care and other items, making employees dependent on the companies; and stagnant wages, which stood at around 60 cents an hour from 1943 to the end of the war. Some companies were already moving away from the paternalism that marked early plantations. Hapco had reallocated most company houses to a non-profit organization that rented them for cash and for a period offered to drop perquisites in return for a 15-cent-an-hour pay raise. Some companies expressed willingness to sign union agreements; others did not.

By the middle of 1946, eleven of twelve plantations had been organized by the ILWU. Hawaiian Fruit Packers was not organized, although its president, Randolph Crossley, chaired the Pineapple Industry Negotiating Committee. All nine canneries were organized. Wages were 70 cents an hour for women and 80 cents for men. The year 1946 saw the first pineapple industry contract negotiations.

The union was still weak. Only full-time workers were organized—seasonals and part-timers were not. Jack Hall considered the union strong on Oʻahu, Lānaʻi, and Molokaʻi, but weak on Maui. The union opened negotiations demanding a 35-cent-per-hour raise. In January 1947, the companies offered 8 cents. The union countered at 23.5 cents; Management offered 10 cents. On May 17, the ILWU pineapple negotiating committee authorized a strike vote and assessed union members $5. On July 8, Harry Bridges, the West Coast ILWU leader, cut the union demand to 15 cents. The parties were near agreement on most points, and the union hinted that if management granted a retroactive raise of 10 cents across the board, with some changes in classification, it might settle. A major point of contention remaining was the length of the contract—the termination dates were four months apart. Shortly after midnight on July 10, ILWU leader Robert McElrath announced on the radio that the union would strike. Management negotiators immediately withdrew all offers.

The 1947 pineapple strike was weak from the start. All the canneries were operating within five days. Hapco was able to run five of its forty-six canning lines and had five hundred of its four thousand people on the job. The company ran all its noisy equipment, even though most wasn't staffed, so the sound of the busy factory would demoralize the strikers. Libby ran six of fourteen lines with two hundred fifty of eight hundred fifty workers. CPC was able to run six of its twenty-four lines with one hundred ten people. The strike was strongest on Lāna'i, but on other islands, volunteers, hundreds of regular workers and part-timers, harvested fruit.

There was also some violence during the strike. On July 11, six hundred strikers stopped three pineapple trucks and forced the drivers to run for safety. When supervisors on Lāna'i tried to operate equipment, workers broke through security lines to stop them. At Lāna'i's Kaumalapau Harbor, three hundred workers chased the crane operator from his rig into the harbor. On the final day of the strike, two Lāna'i truck drivers were beaten.

The pineapple industry's first strike ended July 16. The companies agreed to raises of 10 cents an hour, some classification changes for merit, and dropped a proposal for a 5 cent wage differential on Kaua'i. The settlement was made retroactive—four months. It covered five thousand field workers and twenty-two hundred in the canneries. The workers on average received $80 in back pay from the agreement, and the deal would cost the companies an additional $1.5 million annually.

The union and companies negotiated subsequent contracts in August 1947, February 1948, and January 1949, when a contract provided for a medical plan in which the companies paid half the employee's medical insurance coverage.

Labor-company relations were often rancorous during the post-war period, but not always industry-wide. For example, all the worker units except the Lānaʻi unit approved the 1950 contract, a two-year pact. The Lānaʻi workers, led by Pedro de la Cruz, rejected it 618 to 33, and on February 27, 1951, 752 Lānaʻi pineapple workers walked out, demanding 12 cents an hour instead of the 8 cents the contract specified. They also wanted a closed shop, job security, and an overhaul of job classifications.

Pineapple is loaded by cable crane at the old Kolo Wharf on Molokaʻi's leeward western shore.

It was a long strike. The union maintained a soup kitchen, and the strikers hunted and fished to supplement food supplies. Hapco was firm. The company said it was willing to hold out through the 1951 harvesting season and take the losses. It was largely a quiet strike, although there were reports of gunfire at spray planes that flew in from Maui to fertilize the fields. The workers stayed out 120 days. The ILWU insisted that any agreement to settle the Lāna'i strike be made industry-wide. The union did not want different plantation-by-plantation contracts.

Ultimately, management agreed to increase the contract pay by 4 to 5 cents an hour over the previously agreed 8 cents, across the industry. The deal was settled at the Waikīkī Tropics September 10 between Employer's Council head Jim Blaisdell and the ILWU's Jack Hall and Louis Goldblatt. The central parties got together the next day at a party at Blaisdell's Kāhala home. They included, among others, Henry White and Neil Cardagan of Hapco, L. Verne Hass of Libby, Jack Driver of Del Monte, and Jack Hall and Louis Goldblatt of the ILWU.

The men feared that Lāna'i's workers would object to having been the lone unit to carry the burden of a strike that benefited the entire industry, but on September 13, 1951 they approved the contract and the next day returned to the fields, which were full of the season's fruit, rotting and were waist-high in weeds.

Labor relations remained strained through the 1950s, but were less difficult than during the early organization days. There were no more pineapple strikes during the 1950s, but the industry was affected by strikes that tied up the docks in 1948, 1949, and 1952. The inability to ship the crop meant lost markets, and shortages of supplies like tin plate for cans, fertilizer, and pesticides. Some canneries secretly transported pineapple barges from Hawai'i to small West Coast ports. One was successfully unloaded in Tillamook, Oregon, but a Hapco barge was prevented from unloading at Tacoma, Washington. The tug pulled its barge north to the Columbia River, but ILWU members from Portland stopped it once more, ultimately destroying some harbor equipment and dumping part of the cargo into the river.

A sixty-one-day walkout in 1968 was the longest industry-wide strike. By this time, several plantations were gone and foreign competition was on the rise. Workers employed passive resistance strategies that would become the hallmark of the late 1960s in protests of various kinds. One technique: CPC workers on Moloka'i lay down on the manager's driveway so he couldn't drive to his office. In contrast to the 1947 strike, the industry was completely shut down. Even long-term field experiments by the plantations' researchers were halted, affecting results for years afterward.

In February 1974, a field and plant strike lasted twenty-two days. Later, a strike at Dole's can-manufacturing plant hurt both Dole and Del Monte, which both bought cans from the plant. Once the cans ran out, Dole processed its fruit into juice and ion-exchange sugar, and shipped it to the Mainland in wooden bins with plastic linings.

During the post-war period, workers made remarkable strides in improving their labor conditions. In 1943, before general organization, pineapple workers were paid 60 cents an hour. Under the first contract, in which men made 10 cents an hour more than women, the employees received double-digit increases. Today, Hawai'i's agricultural workers are the highest-paid in the world. For the workers, that's been good. But for the Hawai'i pineapple industry, which competes internationally with firms that pay much less, it's been a problem. In 1990, field workers in Tanzania were paid one percent of Hawaiian wages. By 1995, world market share for Hawaiian pineapple dropped from a high of 85 percent to less than 10 percent, and Hawai'i's industry deteriorated from the post war 12 plantations and 9 canneries to 3 plantations and one cannery.

Store display markets Hawaiian pineapple under a placard depicting flower leis and hula girls.

Exodus

C ommercial pineapple in Hawai'i peaked in acreage in 1957 at 76,700 acres, and packed in production in 1955 at 1,048,000 tons of fruit. This was a dramatic rise from the 5,368 fruits that were first exported at the industry's start in 1891. In 1894 exportation was up to 50,000 fruit. The first pack, by Hawaiian Fruit and Packing Company, was 486 cases in 1895, and 5,000 cases the next year. Fresh fruit exports reached 117,000 in 1897.

Pineapple production spread to nearly every Hawaiian island. Only areas with shipping, climate, or other problems fell by the wayside. Maui, O'ahu, Moloka'i, Lāna'i, and Maui remained major pineapple producers, but by 1969, Kaua'i Pineapple Company, Hawaiian Canneries, Grove Farm, Baldwin Packers, Libby on Maui, and Pacific Pineapple Company were out of the business. Total acreage was down to 62,400, a 17 percent drop from the peak in the previous decade. By 1989 acreage had shrunk to 33,000 acres. Dole's closing of Lāna'i pineapple operations in 1992 cut it to 16,000 acres, of which a third was dedicated to fresh fruit sales. In 1973, Hawai'i still produced 33 percent of the world's canned pineapple, but 30 years later the figure would be hovering at 5 percent.

Although Hawai'i growers found it difficult to compete in the canned pineapple market, they were still strong players in the fresh fruit market. They produced high quality fruit and had good distribution systems to bring it to market. The Islands controlled 51 percent of the United States fresh fruit market in 1986. The figure may now have dropped 5 percent with the advent of Del Monte's new operation in Costa Rica and Dole's plantations in Honduras and the Dominican Republic. However the drop in percentage was not because of reduced production from Hawai'i. Rather, it was because the market on the East Coast had grown, which is primarily supplied by the Central American plantations. The California market remains a strong one for pineapple, and Hawaiian pine can be expected to continue producing crop for that market for years to come, probably utilizing between 10,000 to 12,000 acres.

The foreign pineapple production initially developed as companies looked for locations that were free of the mealybug-spread pineapple wilt in the late 1920s and early 1930s. Until Walter Carter developed a means of controlling it, the disease threatened to destroy Hawaiian pineapple. Meanwhile, the three largest companies aggressively moved abroad.

Dole positioned itself for a short time in Fiji. Although the pineapple cannery survived there for several decades, Dole was out of the business in Fiji by 1932.

Del Monte went into the Philippines in 1926 and started what would become the largest pineapple plantation in the world, which continues to operate today.

Libby investigated the Philippines, North Borneo, the Malay states and Sumatra in 1926, the West Indies, South and

Pineapple can label.

Central America in 1929, Tanganyika, and Kenya in 1929 and 1930. In 1930, Libby selected two trial sites and secured options on two large sections of land in Kenya. L.T. Lyman planted and harvested the two areas. However, the effort was soon abandoned, due to the 1931 depression, the control of the wilt, and improving yields in Hawai'i where planting practices changed from 7,800 to 17,000 plants per acre. The plants left behind in Kenya later became the core foundation of Kenya Canners, the forerunner of Del Monte's Kenyan operation.

A number of non-U.S. companies were competing with Hawai'i as well. After World War II, pineapple was canned in Mexico, the Philippines, Malaysia, South Africa, Australia (for domestic consumption only), and eventually in Taiwan, Thailand, Kenya, China, and Indonesia. During the last few decades, plantations aimed primarily at producing pineapples

PERCENT OF WORLD PRODUCTION OF BOTH CANNED AND FRESH PINEAPPLE.

Location/Year	`42	50	60	70	80	90	00
Hawai'i	83	51	36	16	6	5	2
Puerto Rico	2	3	2	1	0	0	0
Cuba	3	7	4	0	0	0	0
Mexico	0	10	7	5	6	4	4
Brazil	0	13	10	8	5	10	9
Colombia	0	0	2	2	1	3	2
Philippines	war	4	5	4	9	10	11
Thailand	0	0	9	4	34	17	17
Taiwan	8	3	6	5	*	*	*
Indonesia	0	0	0	1	2	3	3
Malaysia	war	2	5	6	2	2	1
Bangladesh	0	0	0	2	1	1	1
China*	0	0	0	7	3	6	9
Vietnam	0	0	2	3	3	4	2
Kenya	0	0	0	1	2	2	2
Ivory Coast	0	0	0	2	3	2	2
S. Africa	2	2	5	3	2	2	1
Cameroon	0	0	0	0	0	0	0
Congo**	0	0	0	1	0	0	0
Congo/Zaire	0	0	0	3	1	1	1
Australia	2	4	3	2	1	1	1
India				7	5	8	8
Nigeria				11	6	7	6
Venezuela				1	1	1	3
Costa Rica				0	0	1	3
Peru				1	0	1	1
Ecuador				1	1	1	1
Honduras				0	0	1	1
Tanzania				1	0	1	1
Guatemala				0	0	1	1
Japan				1	1		

*China's figure excludes Taiwan in the early years, but includes it after 1970; **Congo Republic is the former French colony Congo-Brazzaville. Congo/Zaire, also called the Congo, is the former Belgian colony Congo-Leopoldville. Its capitol is now called Kinshasa.

In 2000, more than 70 counties were listed with the United Nations Food and Agriculture Administration as producing pineapple, but production in most cases was quite small. Nations that achieved one percent of world production in no more than one year include Cambodia, Dominican Republic, El Salvador, Ghana, Guinea, Madagascar, Paraguay, and Sri Lanka.

PERCENT OF WORLD PRODUCTION, CANNED FRUIT ONLY.

Location/Year	`42	50	60	70	80	90	00
Hawai'i	83	74	55	37	16	1	0
Puerto Rico	2	1	1	1	0	0	0
Cuba	3	4	2	0	0	0	0
Mexico	0	0	0	0	0	0	0
Philippines	war	4	7	10	22	19	25
Thailand	0	0	6	10	32	43	44
Ryukyu Isls.	war	0	1	2	1	0	0
Taiwan	8	5	9	10	4	*	*
Indonesia	0	0	0	4	5	5	13
Malaysia	war	3	7	8	3	6	1
China*	0	0	0	3	3	3	2
Kenya	0	0	1	1	3	7	6
Ivory Coast	0	0	1	3	4	0	0
Swaziland	0	0	0	0	1	2	1
South Africa	2	3	6	5	2	3	3
Australia**	2	6	4	5	3	0	0
Netherlands	0	0	0	0	0	1	3
Singapore	0	0	0	0	0	5	2
Belgium	0	0	0	0	0	0	1
Germany	0	0	0	0	0	0	2

*China excludes Taiwan, except after 1990; **Australian production is entirely used within the country; *** More than 70 counties are listed in United Nations records as canning pineapple, but the majority produce very little and individually produce less than one percent of world production. Those with half a percent or less of world canning are not listed here.

NOTE: Due to rounding, numbers may not add up to 100 percent.

for the fresh fruit market have appeared in Honduras, Costa Rica, Brazil, Colombia, along the Ivory Coast, as well as other areas. Taiwan became a formidable competitor but its production has waned to less than 5 percent of world pineapple production.

Del Monte moved into the Philippines in 1926 when the mealybug wilt was hitting Hawaiian pineapple. Other companies closed their foreign operations when the wilt was controlled, but Del Monte continued their international operations. They grew the crop in the province of Bukidnon on the island of Mindanao. The area is 10 degrees north of the equator, and Del Monte found that this higher elevation made for good pineapple growing. The rainfall of 100 inches a year was well distributed throughout the year and the soils well drained. During World War II the plantation suffered dramatically and the cannery was virtually destroyed. However, immediately after the war, the jungle was knocked back and the company replanted pineapple on 15,000 of the 20,000 acres it leased from the government.

The Del Monte company is called Philippines Packing Corporation, PPC, and it has added a cattle operation that uses pineapple byproducts as cattle feed. Fresh pineapple from the PPC plantation is aimed primarily at the Japan market. The plantation produces more than 10 percent of the world canned pineapple market and 60 percent of Del Monte's total production.

Del Monte bought Kenya Canners, near Thika in Kenya, in the 1960s. The plantation had been started with leftovers from Libby's early 1930s experimental plantings. Del Monte built a modern cannery. The firm leases 7,500 acres from the government. Conditions are on the cool side, but the fruit is generally of high quality.

The company started a fresh fruit operation in Costa Rica in the 1970s, intending to supply the eastern United

States. Roughly 6,000 acres are planted, and the fields can be expanded to 8,000 acres. Del Monte has a cooling plant for the fresh fruit and a concentrate plant to process juice from fruit not suited for sale as fresh fruit. The Costa Rica plantation is a major player in the eastern United States fresh pineapple market.

Dole investigated several areas of southeast Asia and the Caribbean, but in 1973 moved into the Philippines, taking up land in Polomok, on the southern west coast of Mindanao, 650 miles south of Manila. Dole gained control over 22,110 acres, with 18,000 of it farmable. The development cost, more than $50 million, was considerably more than the company anticipated. Dole shipped its first planting material to the Philippines from its Lāna'i plantation. Dolefil's, as the operation is called, 1974 ratoon crop, failed apparently because of a planting experiment. The company reportedly spaced the plants closer together than normal, in order to reduce the size of the large fruits of the first crop. However, the second, or ratoon, crop is normally smaller than the first, and the experiment resulted in a ratoon crop whose fruit was undersized.

Dole bought a small company in Thailand in 1974, but had to overcome numerous obstacles, including moving squatters from the land and leveling land that had many undrainable areas. The company had hoped for production of 150,000 tons of fruit annually, and eventually approached that figure with production from its own fields added to extensive purchases from other growers. Dole Thailand now supplies about 6 percent of the world's canned pineapple.

The Honduras Dole plantation started in the 1960s, producing primarily fresh fruit from 6,000 acres. It also produced concentrate from fruits unsuitable for sale as fresh fruit: But the land was rocky, making mechanical operations difficult, and rainy, overcast conditions created soft fruits subject to disease and bruising. Dole sold the plantation to local interests in the 1980s, although it continues to market the fruit.

Dole started an operation in the northern part of the Dominican Republic in the early 1980s. This plantation now supplies a good part of Dole's fresh fruit marketed in the eastern United States.

Libby, McNeill & Libby had experimented in Kenya in the early 1930s, but didn't aggressively move abroad again until the 1960s. In 1964, the company arranged with a French firm to investigate the potential for pineapple in the Republic of Congo, then known as the French Congo or Congo-Brazzaville. The Congo's political climate was deteriorating by the mid-1960s, and the Libby abandoned its experiments there in 1966.

As the company was closing down the last of its Hawai'i plantations, Libby bought a small pineapple operation in Swaziland in 1969. The southern African location did not prove to be good for pineapple—low winter temperatures caused plants to mature slowly. Thus, the Swaziland fields required five years to get through a two-crop cycle that normally took just three years in Hawai'i. Despite this, low land and labor costs made the plantation profitable, and it was able to finance its own expansion in its early years.

Libby-Swaziland, by then known as Swaziland Fruit Canners, was sold in 1983 to South African interests. The plantation is still in operation. Libby, however, is not. Owned by Nestlé, Libby was dissolved in the 1980s and surviving parts of its operations were absorbed by subsidiaries of its parent firm.

Stokely-Van Camp, which was the exclusive distributor for the products of Hawaiian Fruit Packers' operation on Kaua'i from 1939 to the plantation's closing in 1973, was active in Puerto Rican pineapple for a time. The largest of the three

Puerto Rican canneries was started in 1957. Dorsey Edwards, former manager of Hawaiian Fruit Packers on Kaua'i, ran the facility for Stokely, but the operation survived only a few years. Dewitt McCloskey, formerly of Libby, managed the cannery for a period for its then owner, the Puerto Rican government. Puerto Rican pineapple reached its peak in 1945, when it produced 8 percent of world production, but today its role internationally is negligible.

None of the foreign pineapple operations, even the largest plantation areas of the Philippines and Thailand, matches the volume and quality that was produced in Hawai'i during its heyday, and given changing market conditions, it's unlikely any ever will. It is difficult to match the Hawaiian climate for good pineapple producing conditions, and much of the international pineapple production occurs in areas where political stability is a problem.

The demand for canned pineapple has diminished, while the market for fresh pineapple flourishes. In order for the product to be of sufficient quality, fresh pineapple must be grown near its markets: Central America and the Caribbean for the eastern United States; Hawai'i for the West Coast; Philippines for Japan; and Central Africa for Europe. As a result, the concentration of pineapple production in one part of the world is unlikely to exist as it once did in Hawai'i, thus Hawai'i's pineapple century will likely never be replaced.

CHAPTER TEN

Adaptation

Hawai'i's residents saw sugar and pineapple decline in tandem—but the declines were not the same. While sugar plunged from being the dominant economic force in the islands to becoming an industry of only two plantations after the turn of the century, the pineapple industry adapted and evolved after a significant decline.

In the early years of the crop, it was a fresh-fruit product, mainly enjoyed by the residents of the Islands where it was grown. Then, for a century, in order to supply the world, the crop was primarily a product for canning plants. At this writing, the last canning plant, located on Maui, is facing severe stress due to both foreign competition and tariffs on the imported steel it uses for the cans. The remainder of the state's crop is grown once again for fresh consumption.

The annual farm value of canned pineapple in the state was about $200 million through the 1980s, ranging from a low of $156 million in 1982 to $203 million in 1987. The value tumbled in the 1990s, settling in the low $70 million to mid-$80 million range. In the first years of the new millennium, the value of canned pineapple had dropped to around $60 million.

However, during this same period, fresh pineapple production rose to stabilize the industry. The fresh market accounted for only $34 million in revenue for the pineapple industry in 1980, climbing to nearly $60 million by the end of that decade. It then continued to climb, reaching $73 million in 2002, more than matching the value of processed, canned pineapple products.

Manufacturers had not given up on the crop and continued innovating even during the decline. In 1984, Del Monte opened its new pineapple juice processing facility at Kunia. And though the industry closed its breeding program at the Pineapple Research Institute in the mid-1980s, by 1989 Del Monte was back with another initiative, its fresh-cut, chilled Hawaiian pineapple product. Consumers concerned about convenience and purity could buy their pineapples fresh, chilled, with the rind already removed, and ready to eat. The product contained no added sugar, acid, or other compounds.

But the juggernaut of international trade could not be defeated. Dole's Lānaʻi plantation, which had been entirely dedicated to canned fruit production, was closed in 1992, and Dole's new owner launched a program to convert the island from an agricultural location to a resort destination.

With the loss of pineapple fields went the canneries. Del Monte closed its cannery in 1985, and Dole cannery in Iwilei closed fruit processing operations in 1991. The Dole cannery structure became a massive retail complex featuring an 18-screen movie theater and a Home Depot store. Maui Pineapple's cannery was the last remaining one operating in the state.

For more than a century, pineapple was Hawaiʻi's premier fruit and second-largest agricultural crop after sugar. By the twenty-first century, it became the state's biggest agricultural crop, surpassing sugar, although that was mostly because of sugar's decline rather than pineapple's growth. The statewide acreage dedicated to pineapple cultivation in 2003 was 16,000. Production of pineapple at the field was 315,000 tons. That is down two-thirds from the 1950s when production exceeded a million tons on nearly 77,000 acres.

The threat of the loss of Maui Pineapple Company's canning operation loomed large as the new century began. The company had been on the edge for at least a decade. In the decade from 1992 to 2001, according to figures from the Securities and Exchange Commission, it lost money in as many years as it made a profit. Foreign-grown canned pineapple was flooding the market, driving prices down. The company got a small reprieve in 1995 when the U.S. government penalized a Thai canned pineapple company for illegally dumping its fruit on the market at below its cost of production, a technique often used to drive competitors out of business. The penalty duties paid by buyers of Thai pineapple propped up the price, giving Maui Pineapple a small profit for four years running. But as the dumping penalties were reduced and other international pineapple growing areas increased production, the pressure returned. Maui Pine began losing money again.

As if the company wasn't facing enough, the federal administration then proposed tariffs on foreign steel to protect the U.S. steel industry. Ironically, helping one domestic industry could kill another. Maui Pine could just about break even, its managers said, despite paying agricultural wages many times those paid in Third World pineapple-growing countries, but if it also had to pay more for the steel in its cans, it could break the company. Maui Pine sought an exemption from the import tariffs.

The loss of the canning operation could have a dramatic impact on the size of the remaining industry. Canned fruit and juice represent nearly half the value of the industry to the state of Hawai'i. In 1996 the value of fresh sales was $68.8 million and the value of canned fruit and juice was $78.2 million. By 1999 the numbers were about even at just more than $72 million each. In 2000, the figures had reversed, with fresh value at $71.4 million and canned at $60.8 million, and in subsequent years, fresh-fruit value continued to outpace canned.

In the summer of 2002, Maui Pine dodged the steel bullet by gaining an exemption from the steel tariffs so that it could continue to buy steel at affordable prices from mills in Japan.

Meanwhile, other issues still face the pineapple industry. The era of using strong chemicals to protect the crop from insects and disease is ending, largely because the side-effects of those chemicals are being better understood. Researchers are working at both the University of Hawai'i and the Agricultural Research Center to use techniques that will make the chemicals unnecessary. Breeding resistant varieties, using cutting-edge genetic engineering technology, is one of the solutions.

At the low-tech end of the spectrum, researchers at the University of Hawai'i's College of Tropical Agriculture and Human Resources are studying techniques such as composting to improve pineapple yields. This is another irony. For many years, the standard practice was to remove any vegetable material from the fields for fear it could spread disease. Pineapple growers burned their fields in part to get rid of unwanted vegetative material. Now, researchers are working on bringing rotted vegetation into the fields as compost to improve growing conditions.

The continuing research effort is another sign that obituaries for pineapple in Hawai'i are premature. Cultivation techniques, varieties, packaging, and marketing are all changing, but Hawai'i seems linked with the crowned fruit. The sweet, familiar flavor of the pineapple and flatlands covered with regular rows of spiky plants continue. This crop, so perfectly suited to the growing conditions found in Hawai'i, is finding ways to survive.

'Ukulele-playing television personality Arthur Godfrey samples the product he sells during a promotional tour in Honolulu.

Crews hoe weeds in Oʻahu pineapple fields in 1943. Note many wear long-sleeved palaka-fabric jackets for protection from the spines on the leaves.

Cultivating Pineapples

Before going into details of growing pineapples, let's discuss a little information about the climate pineapples prefer.

First, temperatures. Pineapple does best when the daily temperature cycle ranges between 68 degrees Fahrenheit and 87 degrees Fahrenheit. In areas where optimum maximum temperatures prevail, the optimal minimum ones are not often encountered.

Temperatures over 96 degrees Fahrenheit are often associated with sunburn of the fruit, although that is a factor of solar radiation rather than temperature. If the day temperatures average below 50 degrees Fahrenheit, very little growth occurs, and growth virtually stops altogether below 46 degrees Fahrenheit. Night temperatures may go to 32 degrees Fahrenheit without any damage, and under certain circumstances, pineapple plants can withstand freezing temperatures. Research found that:

• At 29.5 degrees Fahrenheit for 1 hour, there was no damage to the plant;
• At 28.0 degrees Fahrenheit for 1 hour, there was only some damage to the plant;
• At 28.0 degrees Fahrenheit for 3 hours or 27.0 degrees Fahrenheit for 1 hour there was appreciable plant damage;
• At 27.0 degrees Fahrenheit for 3 hours or 26.0 degrees Fahrenheit for 1 hour, plant damage was drastic;

- At 25.5 degrees Fahrenheit for 1 hour, there was complete destruction, although 67 percent of the plants regrew from later development of ground suckers;
- If the plants are protected by overhead irrigation (at ¼-inch per hour), the plant damage at all these combinations was negligible;
- If the plants were covered with fiber cloth (marketed for this purpose) or any other cloth (but definitely not plastic), the lighter damage is eliminated and the heavier damage to the plants is considerably reduced, depending on the thickness of the cover.
- If fruit that is within four weeks of harvest is only protected from frost by irrigation, it may show inter-eye cracking (very small but deep cracks) from being subjected to less than one hour exposure to 29 degrees Fahrenheit.

At home, normal room temperatures should be fine to grow pineapple plants, especially if the night temperatures are somewhat moderate.

Second, let's address water use. A pineapple plant should not be over-watered, especially if it is planted in a poorly drained medium. Pineapples are plants of semi-desert habitats. From planting time to the first visible start of growth, a pineapple plant needs 0.08 inch of water daily. In Hawai'i, that works out to just less than 5 inches of water over a two-month period. Thereafter, if the water application is well distributed, 0.75 inch per week suffices unless there is a fast-drying soil medium. Plants will likely do poorly under these conditions: 3 months or more with less than 0.5 inch per month; 4 months or more with less than 1.0 inch per month; 5 months or more with less than 1.5 inches per month.

Third, a pineapple's light requirements. In commercial pineapple growing areas (roughly between 20 degrees north and 20 degrees south of the equator) day lenghts cause no difficulty in the development of pineapple, except in places with extended periods of overcast skies (where, among other things, problems from disease may develop). At home the plant should have all the daylight possible, especially during winter in more temperate latitudes. Serious amateurs may want to consider artificial lighting, such as "Grow-Lux" lights, to extend the day to 12 hours.

VARIETIES

There are many pineapple varieties, but unless you make an effort at collecting, you are most likely to encounter the following four:

• Smooth Cayenne is so common that it may be the only variety most people know. It is a nice looking plant with only a few spines at the leaf tips. The acidity and sugar of the fruit are higher than in most other varieties, and the combination makes for a very good, crisp taste.

• Queen is a favorite in South Africa and was once grown abundantly in Florida. Its leaves are quite spiny, making it less desirable for cultivation at home. The plant and fruit are smaller than Smooth Cayenne. Sugar and acid are also somewhat lower, but the fruit, though less juicy, has a pleasant aroma and flavor. The Queen variety is considered less decorative than the Smooth Cayenne.

• Red Spanish, which we find mostly in Puerto Rico today, is intermediate in size between Smooth Cayenne and Queen. The leaves are long and very spiny. The fruit is fibrous with pale yellow flesh, and, while the flavor is quite different from the others, it is rather pleasant. The plant looks good and is very hardy, but it is not recommend for use at home because of the spines.

• Manzana, which is a favorite in Colombia and is sometimes exported to the U.S, has plants which are somewhat darker green and more purplish than Smooth Cayenne, but otherwise they are quite similar. The fruit is pleasant tasting, rather round-shaped with a purple tinge. It has somewhat more spines than Smooth Cayenne but it is more susceptible to freezing damage. As a houseplant it is prefered it over Queen and Red Spanish but not over Smooth Cayenne.

THE GROWING CYCLE

The speed of plant growth and fruit development is relative to the day temperatures to which the plant is exposed. In South Africa a cycle of two crops takes 47 months, while in Hawai'i it takes only an average of 33 months. Below are the cycle periods for various areas:

Location; Cycle lengths in months to first crop; first to second crop
Martinique, Taiwan, Hawai'i: 20; 13
Fiji, Ceylon, Malaya: 18; 8
Brazil, Philippines: 13; 8
South Africa, Swaziland: 29; 18

If a plant is grown at home, near a window, with the mean temperature kept at, say, 76–78 degrees Fahrenheit, the cycle length should be somewhere like that of Hawai'i crops: planting to (induced) budding, 13 months; budding to plant crop (first) harvest, 7 months; first harvest to ratoon (second) crop's (induced) bud, 6 months; ratoon budding to ratoon harvest, 7 months. Total time for two crops, 33 months.

COMPOSITION OF PLANT AND FRUIT

A description of the plant's parts from the bottom upwards: there are the roots, then the plant's stump, the peduncle or the stem of the fruit, then the fruit and crown. A plant sends out side shoots in two areas. A sucker is the name for a shoot growing from the plant's thick stump, and a slip is a shoot growing from the thinner peduncle.

GROWING YOUR OWN

There are several ways to get started. In many areas, you can buy a fruited or non-fruited plant in a pot. But it's less expensive to buy a pineapple fruit at the grocery store and plant its crown. When buying this fruit you must make sure that the crown's heart has not been destroyed, which is sometimes done by growers to limit the crown size. This is done before harvest by either destroying the crown's growing-point with a metal scoop or by dropping some types of acid into the crown heart. Sometimes, in the packing house, large crowns are reduced in size by twisting-out the center part. If the center of the plant's crown appears damaged, it is not suitable for planting.

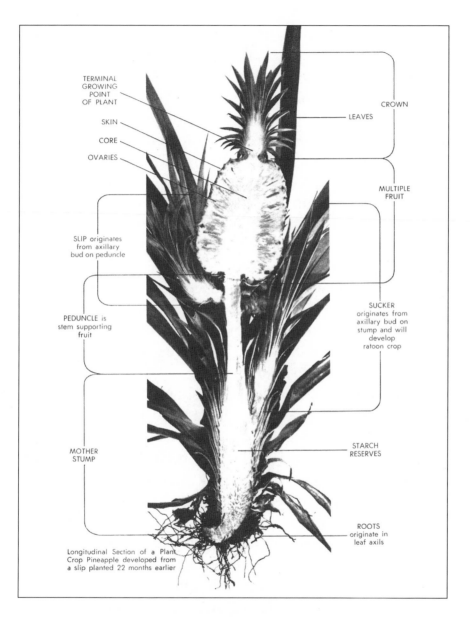

TERMINAL
GROWING
POINT
OF PLANT

CROWN

SKIN

LEAVES

CORE

OVARIES

MULTIPLE
FRUIT

SLIP originates
from axillary
bud on peduncle

PEDUNCLE is
stem supporting
fruit

SUCKER
originates from
axillary bud on
stump and will
develop
ratoon crop

MOTHER
STUMP

STARCH
RESERVES

ROOTS
originate in
leaf axils

Longitudinal Section of a Plant
Crop Pineapple developed from
a slip planted 22 months earlier

Cutaway view of the pineapple plant.

If you're buying a pineapple in a pot, just pick up the growing cycle at the stage at which the plant is potted. The planting medium can be soil, sand (but not coral sand), vermiculite, peat, a mixture of any of these, or even plain water to which nutrients are added (hydroponics). A light soil or sand mixed with peat in equal proportions or a mixture of one part vermiculite with four parts of potting soil is recommended.

For planting material you can use crowns, slips, suckers, or even the stump. It is also possible to expand the number of starting plants by cutting crowns, slips, suckers, or the stump into sections, although this slows the amount of time before plants reach fruiting size.

Slips and suckers are preferred planting materials, but if you are growing pineapples for the first time, these probably won't be available to you, so use the crown of a store-bought fruit. You can plant the crown whole for fastest maturity, or you can cut it into halves or quarters.

To section a crown into halves, first trim the top of the crown, leaving a base section of about four inches from the butt to the cut. Then cut them longitudinally, that is, from top to bottom, leaving two identical sides, and plant them each directly into three-gallon plastic pots. Expect that one half will develop much faster than the other (one half will develop directly into a plant while the other half will develop a sucker which will be the future plant). If the crown's diameter is greater than 1 1/4 inches, it can be sectioned once more, into quarters. To section a crown into quarters, cut the halves again lengthwise.

The sections are planted at an angle with the cut side down and leaves up. Plant sections four to six inches apart in a mixture of half sand and half peat, with fertilizer added in. Be sure there are drain holes in the bottom of the planting box.

If it's available, use 15-3-15 fertilizer, preferably with

about 1 percent magnesium, 1 percent iron, and 1 percent manganese. In most complex fertilizers, you'll find three numbers. The first applies to the percentage of nitrogen in the mix; the second, phosphate, and the third, potassium. The higher the numbers, the stronger the fertilizer. Check the labels, since many household fertilizers also contain micronutrients such as magnesium, iron, manganese, and others. Many fertilizers also have some of the fertilizer immediately available to the plants and some in slow-release form. These simplify the home grower's work, since they reduce the number of fertilizer applications required.

It will take several weeks for the sections to develop tiny plants. They will appear from buds between the leaves. When the new plants are about four inches high, you can pull them up and plant them in three-gallon pots. To do so, simply push them into the pot's planting medium and apply water to settle the medium around the base of the new plant.

If you are planting a whole crown, be sure to trim the moist flesh off the base of the crown and then leave the crown on its side or standing upside down for a few days to dry. This will help prevent rotting. Strip off leaves at the base of the crown, revealing a half inch or so of core. You'll see small bumps on the core. These will develop into roots. When ready, press the crown down into the planting medium. At planting time, add three grams, or about half a teaspoon, of the fertilizer mix mentioned above, to the top of the medium in the three-gallon pot. If you can't locate the 15-3-15 formula, you can decrease or increase the rate according to the difference (i.e., for 5-1-5, use three times as much).

Pineapples don't need a lot of water, but you should irrigate your plants so the medium is moist and doesn't completely dry out. As long as the pot's base has drainage holes and isn't standing in water, there is not much chance of damaging the plants from over watering.

Fertilize either monthly at three grams per three-gallon pot, or use 9 grams every three months. It's useful to make a note on your calendar so you don't lose track of the fertilizing schedule. Discontinue the fertilizer applications when the red bud of the fruit is visible at the plant's center and has a diameter of one inch. Resume fertilizing after harvesting the fruit, and continue until the largest sucker displays a one-inch fruit bud. All suckers except the largest should be snapped off the plant as soon as they are noticed.

A variety of pests may interfere with the growth of your pineapple plant. For weed control, simply pull out any that appear. If your growing medium is clean, there should be few or no weeds, but since soil often contains weed seeds, it can produce a somewhat larger problem.

Mealybugs, white fluffy insects about one eighth of an inch in diameter, attach themselves to the leaves and sometimes to the roots and base of the fruit. One solution is to spray the plant thoroughly with an insecticide. A solution of 1 teaspoon of 55 percent Malathion in one-third of a gallon of water will do the trick. If you prefer, simply spray the plant with a soap-and-water mixture.

For scale insects, very small gray-white discs attached to the leaves, we recommend simply wiping the affected leaves with a light solution of soapy water.

The plants should not suffer from diseases such as fungus attacks if they are grown in well-drained media and water is applied appropriately. Either too much or too little water can cause problems. The most prevalent fungal agent is phytophthora, which can cause heart and root rot. This fungus thrives in alkaline soil, which has a high pH. The optimum soil pH for pineapple is 5.5, which is slightly acidic. Too much lime or coral sand in the planting medium can raise the soil alkalinity and lead to disease problems. If you're growing pineapple in open soil, take a sample to your local agricultural extension office and have it tested for soil pH. If it's on the alkaline side, you can add ammonium sulfate. For each plant, mix a tablespoon in irrigation water and apply it to the plants.

The plant will produce fruit buds naturally when the plant is big enough and the weather starts to cool down at night, to anywhere from 64 degrees Fahrenheit down to as low as 45 degrees. If there are only a few plants in the house, you can force them to bud by exposing them for one or two nights to low temperatures, down to near 45 degrees.

The plants can also be forced to bud using chemicals. If you can find it, apply half a thimble of calcium carbide to the plant heart and then apply some water. You can ask in garden shops or even a welding shop for this chemical. Apply the calcium carbide late at night or early in the morning. Commercially, pineapples are forced to bud with a chemical called ethrel but the quantity needed for only a few plants would be difficult to measure and to buy a bottle of ethrel at the garden shop for such a minute requirement would be quite uneconomical.

A simple but effective way to force a plant is by covering it with a garbage pail or an improvised plastic tent and then burning some moist tree leaves under the cover, which produces the forcing chemical, ethylene. The phenomenon of ethylene making pineapple plants bud was discovered in the Azores when the growers used plant residue as fuel to heat their pineapple greenhouses. Ripening fruit also produce ethylene, and you can encase your plant in a plastic bag or under a garbage can with a couple of ripening apples for a week and get a similar result.

Pineapple plants do not require much maintenance while the fruit is developing. Fertilizing is stopped. Water is applied as it is through the growing stage. The first major change after you spot the red fruit bud is the flowering of the pineapple. Pale blue flowers will sprout from the bud for two weeks or so. You'll be able to harvest the fruit about seven months after forcing to bud. There will be some variability in how long it takes the fruit to ripen. The fruit is ready when the skin or shell is between three-quarters and completely yellow, although there are conditions where the fruit is ripe when almost still completely green. An alternative method of checking whether the fruit is ripe requires that we snap a finger against the shell at the center of the fruit. If this produces a dull, solid (rather than a hollow) sound, the fruit is ripe. This procedure may take some practice and one can achieve experience by practicing with the pineapples in a store's produce department.

NOTES ON SUBSEQUENT CROPS

During fruit development of the first crop, called the plant crop or mother crop, one or more suckers start developing from the plant's stem. Suckers can also start after the first harvest. After harvest, remove all visible suckers except the largest one. (The removed suckers can be planted, and will produce a new fruit crop.) This sucker will produce the second, or ratoon crop. The ratoon fruit is produced in about half the time that it took to get from planting to the first crop.

The ratoon fruit will be smaller than the plant crop, and if the additional suckers are not removed, the fruit size will be further reduced. If you leave a second sucker on, and it also fruits, both fruits will be dramatically reduced in size. If left to

Slips are removed from the plants and piled in groups of ten for a two-week drying period. They will be used for planting new fields.

continue growing, the sucker that produced the ratoon crop can produce its own suckers, but if this is allowed, the fruits will be even smaller, roughly the size of a tennis ball. The author has seen plants at high elevation on the island of Sumatra in Indonesia that produced a seventh ratoon with an acceptable fruit size but we can't expect to match those conditions anywhere in the United States, particularly in a living room. Most commercial growers replant the fields after the first ratoon crop, using whole slips, suckers, or crowns. That's a good practice for home growers as well.

Index

Index

Index